Michael Paffard

The Unattended Moment

Excerpts from Autobiographies
with Hints and Guesses

SCM PRESS LTD

by the same author

Inglorious Wordsworths
*A Study of Some Transcendental Experiences
in Childhood and Adolescence*
(Hodder & Stoughton 1973)

334 01721 1
First published 1976
by SCM Press Ltd
56 Bloomsbury Street London WC1

© SCM Press Ltd 1976

Printed in Great Britain by
Richard Clay (The Chaucer Press) Ltd
Bungay, Suffolk

The Unattended Moment

*For most of us, there is only the unattended
Moment, the moment in and out of time,
The distraction fit, lost in a shaft of sunlight,
The wild thyme unseen, or the winter lightning
Or the waterfall, or music heard so deeply
That it is not heard at all, but you are the music
While the music lasts. These are only hints and guesses,
Hints followed by guesses.*

T. S. Eliot
The Dry Salvages

Contents

Acknowledgments

My first debt of gratitude is to the authors, excutors and publishers who have given permission to quote from copyright material. Secondly, I want to thank all those correspondents, known and unknown to me, who wrote about my previous book, *Inglorious Wordsworths*, and encouraged me to produce this sequel to it or drew my attention to autobiographical accounts of 'unattended moments': the list is incomplete, but the following spring to mind; David and Jeanne Bolam, L. Casselden, Revd K. G. Chapman, J. W. P. Creber, Basil DeMel, C. J. Gill, Professor Sir Alister Hardy, G. L. Heawood, Professor M. V. C. Jeffreys, Marghanita Laski, Professor J. J. Lawlor, E. W. Lighton, D. W. Menzies, Dr Ian Michael, Enid and Gerry Nussbaum, Mrs D. O. Pym, E. A. Robinson, Desmond Vowles and Mrs G. J. Warnock. Finally, I am once more indebted to Mrs R. Wilkes for her care in typing my manuscript and to the library staff at the University of Keele for help in obtaining many books.

Introduction

As a boy I collected all manner of objects, shells and fossils
and pressed flowers and minerals, even feathers and skulls,
and found much satisfaction in poring over, arranging and
rearranging my collections. I also enjoyed jig-saw puzzles,
bringing together the scattered interlocking pieces to make a
coherent picture. Making this book has given me similar
satisfactions: it is a collection and also a puzzle. Whether any
coherent pattern emerges, I must leave the reader to judge.
I hope he will at least be rewarded by finding in it some new
pieces which he can build into his own pattern if he does not
like mine. The pattern is not in any case very important: a
shift of the kaleidoscope would produce from the same fragments something quite different and perhaps equally satisfying.

When I arranged those schoolboy collections I was not
generally following any system of classification that would have
made sense to an expert: I was too ignorant. The grouping
was intuitive and aesthetic for children are natural artists but
have to grow up to science. Similarly with this book, the
arrangement should not be supposed to offer anything so
formal as a taxonomy. Distinctions have been argued for; the
extrovertive and introvertive mysticism of Professor W. T.
Stace and Marghanita Laski's three types of ecstasy, the
adamic, the noetic and the unitive representing, in religious
terms, a scale of ascending values. But for my purpose the
kaleidoscope is a good image because what I want to present
is a complicated pattern of reflections and overlapping

similarities rather than neatly docketed specimens and clear-cut distinctions. I have borrowed the title of the book and my chapter headings from T. S. Eliot's *Four Quartets* but I must not be thought to offer, however covertly, a commentary on that great poem, profoundly though it interests me.

After all these disclaimers, what are the specimens in the collection, the pieces of the puzzle? Dr Johnson said, 'A man will turn over half a library to make one book' and that, more or less, is what I have done. It will soon be apparent that the shelves of autobiography and memoir have been most frequently ransacked. And what have I pilfered from other men's memories? That is not so easily answered: *moments* certainly; brief flashes of experience, often but not always in childhood or adolescence and so out-of-the-ordinary as to seem to belong to a dimension other than the quotidian, to be epiphanies of another order of reality: *unattended* moments in the sense that they do not seem to fit into our ordinary pattern of experience and are therefore difficult to come to terms with, to think about or to communicate. The limits of our language are the limits of our world to the extent that they circumscribe what we can normally think and speak about, but we are aware of another world just outside the limits. 'The Unattended Moment' is a misnomer in that the authors I have quoted in this book are unusual precisely because they *have* attended and *do* find words to talk about experience which is usually inarticulate and therefore unattended.

What I have done in collecting their experiences together scarcely amounts to providing hints and guesses: it has been rather a matter of erecting a framework, a plain setting for those passages which have impressed me as containing echoes of that twilight *terra incognita* beyond the limits where words fail though meanings still exist. What I have written can easily be ignored and the book treated as an unannotated anthology. It may be better so. On the one occasion I visited Chartres Cathedral a fat little French priest with squeaking shoes was conducting a party round the awe-inspiring building. He pointed out this, drew attention to that, rattled off facts and dates, chivied along his unprotesting flock like an officious sheepdog. His voice echoed everywhere, never pausing for a moment to let the sights he was describing speak for themselves in silence. There was no escaping him and his squeaking shoes either; but I do beg the reader of this book, if so inclined, to skip the guide's tiresome rattle which is easily accomplished.

A. E. Housman, who could be a waspish reviewer, once said of a writer that he used quotations as a drunkard uses lampposts, more to support his instability than to illuminate his path. It would be a telling criticism of this book if I had indeed a path to walk, a chalk-line of argument to follow with steps inebriate or sober, a thesis to propound. But the truth is different, as I have already suggested. The book is first a collection of mysterious specimens, and the wanderings they prompted are secondary.

Some people will object, in Forster's words, that 'a mystery is nothing but a high sounding name for a muddle', that speculation is pointless, that all we need is a little patience for surely we are on the verge of understanding the chemical mechanisms of mysticism, the biology of the beatific vision, the pathology of ecstasy and awe and that the mystery will evaporate in the sunlight of science. It may be so, but I am more aware of 'the oppression of the silent fog'. I doubt whether the time is ripe for proofs and certainties. There are few generalizations we can safely make about the unattended moment and exceptions to all of them. They are commoner in youth than in maturity, out of doors than in, in the evening than earlier in the day, and in solitude rather than in company. These are facts, as I showed in an earlier book called *Inglorious Wordsworths*, but tell us little that is worth knowing; the danger always is that 'knowledge imposes a pattern, and falsifies'. When Eliot says this, what he means, I think, is that religious and aesthetic knowledge is existential, not demonstrable like scientific knowledge but part of the individual's experience. If it turns out that a few chemical substances secreted by the glands under certain circumstances, or deliberately ingested, *cause* these experiences, even that information will be of limited interest and fraught with fearful dangers as we already have reason to be aware. The roots of the experience are less important than its fruits, for experiences happen to people and are transformed by their personalities. Every experience is there-

9

fore unique. It would be a supreme irony if, by swallowing a little pill, a man could share the creative vision of the greatest artist or attain that beatitude which a lifetime of religious devotion has rarely achieved. The vision may be necessary but is certainly not sufficient to make an artist or a saint, indeed it may contain the seeds of a dangerous spiritual conceit.

I have said that people transform experiences, whatever their cause, by embodying or, better, by 'personalizing' them; but one of the things that makes the unattended moment important and a subject of our special wonder, is that it does often seem to the people who have it that *it* transforms *them*. They will say, not infrequently, that it has given them new aspirations and a sense of 'possible sublimity', enhanced their ability to love their fellow men, quickened their feeling for both the mystery and the meaningfulness of life, implanted in them an unshakable intuition of a benevolent purpose at work in the world and of the ultimate unity of the good, the true and the beautiful. If these are illusions they are life-enhancing ones and they seem to be commoner, or at least more commonly recorded, than those darker glimpses of the Everlasting No which I have also included in this book.

Unattended moments could be said to be 'caused' by whatever sights, sounds or other stimuli immediately precede them and appear to trigger them off. I believe a study of the passages in this book will show this to be a misleading way of looking at them. Often the 'cause' in this sense is quite un-exceptional, even trivial, and the same set of circumstances will trigger off an experience for one person but not for another or precipitate a 'moment' on one occasion but not on many others. In writing about his hero Stephen's moments or 'epiphanies', James Joyce speaks of 'the significance of trivial things'. I think this is misleading in the same way. Certainly the moment or experience is out of all proportion to the stim-ulus (or any imaginable stimulus) which therefore seems trivial – that is part of the puzzling and paradoxical character of the moment – but what is significant, I suggest, is the subjective mood or exact state of balance of mind and body of the per-son who has the experience. The unattended moment may come when we are travelling in a train, ill in bed, reading a

book or washing the dishes; in the most humdrum surroundings we may be 'surprised by joy'; but even when it
does seem to be triggered off by, for example, a sunset or a
symphony, relatively *objective* considerations such as the
exceptional splendour of the sunset or the perfection of the
performance seem to be less important than the readiness of the
subject. Moreover, if we except the religious disciplines prac-
tised by some holy men, it seems that the unattended moment
can rarely if ever be deliberately induced: we do not know
when it will come because we do not understand what factors
make us ready to step into that other dimension. Like much
else that lies behind the conscious threshold of our minds, the
harder we seek it consciously, the more certainly will it elude
us.

The crucial importance of the subjective holds, I believe,
for a further aspect of the unattended moment. What a person
makes of it and certainly how he describes it if he does attend
to it will be shaped more by his personality than by anything
external to his senses or merely neuro-physiological. At any
moment in time we are a complex of ideas, attitudes, ex-
pectations, needs and desires: to misappropriate a famous
line of Shelley's, we are each of us like domes of many-
coloured glass staining the white radiance of eternity. Of
course, if we have an unattended moment at a concert or in a
picture gallery or while reading a poem we are likely to think
of it as an intense aesthetic experience. Similarly, if the
moment comes in a Cathedral or at some religious ceremony
we shall probably think of it as religious experience. In either
case we may use language more appropriate to the other
in our description: the holiness of beauty and the beauty of
holiness are equally intelligible hyperboles. But if the experience comes in entirely ordinary surroundings, if it is
triggered off by some natural scene with no man-made ex-
pressive intention, if it is a childhood moment only remembered
and put into words many years afterwards, then the beliefs
and ideas the person brings to it will determine what it is
called. It is impossible, I think, wholly to disentangle what an
experience was like from how it is described and the description will be shot through with those ideas and assumptions

about the origin, nature or significance of the experience which William James called 'over-beliefs'. I do not want to argue the point at length here because I have done so in my earlier book but I do think the reader of the following chapters will be struck again and again by the way in which two writers will describe what seem to have been very similar experiences but one will fit it into a religious and the other into an aesthetic frame of reference. Gerardus van de Leeuw in his book *Sacred and Profane Beauty*[1] puts it less clumsily:

> Climb up upon this height and you will see how the paths of beauty and holiness approach each other, growing distant, until finally in the far distance, they can no longer be held apart.

Whether a writer describes the unattended moment as religious or aesthetic he will often say also that it made him feel good, loving, benevolent, altruistic as we shall see particularly in chapter 5. There really does seem to be a mysterious affinity binding together the trinity of religious truths, aesthetic beauty and moral goodness which some readers will have no difficulty in giving a name.

Since this is to be a book of quotations I shall end this Introduction by illustrating the complexity and beauty of the kaleidoscope's pattern from one or two writers. Here first of all is Walter Pater in one of his *Miscellaneous Studies* which we can take to be autobiographical though he writes a third person narrative of a childhood experience.

> I have remarked how, in the process of our brain-building, as the house of thought in which we live gets itself together, like some bird's-nest of floating thistle-down and chance straws, compact at last, little accidents have their consequence; and thus it happened that, as he walked one evening, a garden gate, usually closed, stood open; and lo! within, a great red hawthorn in full flower, embossing heavily the bleached and twisted trunk and branches, so aged that there were but few green leaves thereon – a plumage of tender, crimson fire out of the heart of the dry wood. The perfume of the tree had now and again reached him, in the currents of the wind, over the wall, and he had wondered what might be behind it, and was now allowed to fill his arms with the flowers – flowers enough for all the old blue-china pots along the chimney-piece, making *fête* in the children's room. Was it some periodic moment in the expansion of soul within him, or mere trick of heat in the heavily-laden summer air? But the beauty of the thing struck home

to him feverishly; and in dreams all night he loitered along a magic roadway of crimson flowers . . . Also then, for the first time, he seemed to experience a passionateness in his relation to fair outward objects, an inexplicable excitement in their presence, which disturbed him, and from which he half longed to be free. A touch of regret or desire mingled all night with the remembered presence of the red flowers, and their perfume in the darkness about him; and the longing for some undivined, entire possession of them was the beginning of a revelation to him, growing ever clearer, with the coming of the gracious summer guise of fields and trees and persons in each succeeding year, of a certain, at times seemingly exclusive, predominance in his interests, of beautiful physical things, a kind of tyranny of the senses over him.

Somewhere T. S. Eliot speaks of words as 'the faded poor souvenirs of passionate moments', but in the hands of a master how marvellously they evoke not merely the colour and heavy scent of the red hawthorn blossom but also the child's response to them. 'Little things have their consequences', he says – the equivalent of Joyce's 'significance of trivial things': and the consequence for him was an 'expansion of soul' and a growing passionateness in his response to natural beauty, a predominance in his interests of beautiful physical things. A typical pagan aesthete in the making, one might say, but the story is more complex than that. A rapturous joy in the beauty of the sensible world, whether of nature or art, is seldom a simple unmixed emotion: it disturbed with a 'longing for some undivined, entire possession'.

. . . he . . . began to note with deepening watchfulness, but always with some puzzled, unutterable longing in his enjoyment, the phases of the seasons and of the growing or waning day . . .
So he yielded himself easily to religious impressions, and with a kind of mystical appetite for sacred things; . . . he began to love, for their own sakes, church lights, holy days, all that belonged to the comely order of the sanctuary, the secrets of its white linen, and holy vessels, and fonts of pure water; and its hieratic purity and simplicity became the type of something he desired always to have about him in actual life . . .
For a time he walked through the world in a sustained, not unpleasurable awe, generated by the habitual recognition, beside every circumstance and event of life, of its celestial correspondent.
Sensibility – the desire of physical beauty – a strange biblical awe, which made any reference to the unseen act on him like

solemn music – these qualities the child took away with him, when, at about the age of twelve years, he left the old house . . .[2]

In later years, Pater tells us, when he came upon philosophies and metaphysical speculations and began consciously to construct his own 'house of thought', what he was doing, he says, was really only to 'reinforce what was instinctive in his way of receiving the world'. It is feeling which makes a man think: the moment of the hawthorn tree had life-long and life-shaping consequences. Like many other writers who will be quoted in later chapters, his life spanned the great debate between the church and the Darwinians. A deep scepticism born of that debate, a strong nostalgia for the religion in which he had been reared and a natural receptiveness to the transcendental had to be reconciled. They led him to find in a stoical philosophy and a reverence for art some alternative to the Christian teaching he could no longer believe in as other men were led to explore spiritualism and all aspects of the occult. The search continues as it must for every man who attends to his moments of ecstasy and awe.

From the nineteenth century to the twentieth, from the man of letters to the distinguished scientist, from childhood to adolescence and from the moment of the red hawthorn to the moment of the wild white cherry: in a later chapter I shall quote moments from Sir Julian Huxley's recent *Memories* but in 1927 he analysed the growth of his own natural piety in *Religion without Revelation*.

On Easter Sunday, early in the morning, I got up at daybreak, before anyone else was about, let myself out, ran across to a favourite copse, penetrated to where I knew the wild cherry grew, and there in the spring dew, picked a great armful of the lovely stuff, which I brought back, with a sense of its being an acceptable offering, to the house. Three or four Easters running I remember doing this.

I was fond of solitude and of nature, and had a passion for wild flowers: but this was only a general basis. It will not account for my acting thus on Easter Day, and only then: I never went off gathering wild cherry or any other flowers before breakfast on other days . . . But somehow, it seems, I found Easter Day a holy day. Naturally I was not at that age concerned to enquire very fully why or how it was holy, whether simply because other people regarded it as holy, or because of some intrinsic quality in the day; but it was a fact that it was so to me. That mysterious and sacred quality

14

impressed itself upon my mind, and had a double effect upon my actions. The holy day became as it were a lightning-conductor onto which could be concentrated those apprehensions which a child may have of something transcendent in the beauty of nature, that dim and vague sense of what can best be called holiness in material things. This, in every day intercourse with other children and with grown-ups, is mixed up with so many other sensations and ideas that it is difficult to talk about; the world, even the child's world, inhibits it. But when sanctity is in the air, as at Easter, then it can have free play.

As Huxley says, the sanctity of the day not only drew out his suppressed feelings for 'something transcendent in the beauty of nature' but also lent a special significance to the beauty of the morning, the cherry blossom and the whole pilgrimage. The quality of holiness was experienced not as a state of his own mind but as actually inhering in the beautiful objects.

At a later stage in his development, he says, he enjoyed the chapel services at Eton not merely for their beauty but for 'something which must be called specifically religious', though he rejected at the same time the Christian scheme, theologically considered, as incomprehensible. And then he discovered art.

. . . once the magic doors were opened and my adolescence became aware of literature and art and indeed the whole emotional richness of the world, pure lyric poetry could arouse in me much intenser and more mystical feelings than anything in the Church service.[3]

And so to a final quotation. Will the reader immediately recognize, I wonder, the source of the blissful euphoria this writer is describing?

. . . we are deeply excited. We are shaken or lifted out of our ordinary state of consciousness. Many of our faculties are, for the moment, enhanced. We feel keener perceptions coming into action within us. We are given the use of more than our normal stock of penetrative sympathy: we feel that we can enter into people's feelings and understand the quality of their lives better than ever before.
    Another effect of the drug is that, while it is acting strongly, the whole adventure of mankind upon the earth gains, in our sight, a new momentousness, precariousness and beauty. The new and higher scale of power in ourselves seems to be challenged by an equal increase in the size of the objects on which it is exercised. Living becomes a grander affair than we had ever thought.
    A third effect on the mind is a powerful sense – authentic or

illusory – of being in the presence of extraordinary possibilities. You feel as if new doors of understanding and delight were beginning to open around you. Some sort of mysterious liberation or empowerment seems to be approaching. You are assured, in an unaccountable way, that wonderful enlightenments, still unreceived, are on their way to you, like new stars that are nearing the point in space at which they will come within range of our sight.[4]

The 'drug' is not alcohol nor opium nor LSD nor some imaginary *soma*: it is not some influx of divine grace. Montague is trying to fix and describe, as he says, the sensations that visit us while under the spell of *poetry*. If we did not know this, 'moral' and 'religious' would seem as appropriate words as 'aesthetic' to describe the experience he is trying to put into words. This is why my book is not only a collection but also a puzzle. Doubtless the important questions about religious, moral and aesthetic experience depend upon criteria and distinctions rather than testimonial opulence, but meaningful distinctions can only be derived from studying the kind of specimens I have brought together here and understanding them better than they are understood at present.

1   The Moment of the Rose

The moment of the rose is a moment of intense joy, joy that goes 'beyond any meaning We can assign to happiness'. Bliss, felicity, rapture and jubilation come nearer to being its synonyms than mere enjoyment, happiness or pleasure. One can be happy – one very often is happy in childhood – without being conscious of one's happiness; but joy is a sudden eruption of happiness into the conscious mind, overwhelming at its most intense, sudden, and usually as short lived as a rocket in its burst of splendour. It makes the psalmist cry out 'O come let us sing unto the Lord: let us make a joyful noise' but it may come to the small child whose mind is as innocent of words as it is of concepts like deity. Willa Muir says:

> My first awareness of it came at the age of two, when I was being pushed high in a swing, a small wooden chair slung from the branches of a tree. At the top of my swing I looked up and saw a pattern of green leaves against the blue sky. Boundless delight floated me for one moment up into that sky beside the green leaves, a moment I have never forgotten . . . This 'floating' experience recurred at odd times, always with an uprush of joyousness; I recognised it when it came upon me but took it for granted; there was no need to put it into words.[1]

Elizabeth Hamilton was a little older, four or five. Was her experience also a sudden uprush of joyousness? I guess it probably was.

> Once as I was looking at a calceolaria, fingering the yellow blossom, marvelling at the mouth that opened and shut and the bulbous under-lip speckled with crimson, God was with me in the garden. It was a moment in time and yet out of it. I wanted to prolong it. But I could not. It had passed and I was alone.[2]

Had she already at that age learnt to associate the experience of joy with the name of God or was it the grown-up mind recollecting that made the connection? I do not think we can tell. Possibly the author herself could not have said. It is often an insoluble problem to distinguish what one thought and felt as a child from what one has felt and thought subsequently about memories of childhood. With Mary Austin this problem does not arise:

> I must have been between five and six when this experience happened to me. It was a summer morning, and the child I was had walked down through the orchard alone and come out on the brow of a sloping hill where there were grass and a wind blowing and one tall tree reaching into the infinite immensities of blueness. Quite suddenly, after a moment of quietness there, earth and sky and tree and wind-blown grass and the child in the midst of them came alive together with a pulsing light of consciousness. There was a wild foxglove at the child's feet and a bee dozing about it, and to this day I can recall the swift inclusive awareness of each for the whole – I in them and they in me and all of us enclosed in a warm lucent bubble of livingness. I remember the child looking everywhere for the source of this happy wonder, and at last she questioned – 'God?' – because it was the only awesome word she knew. Deep

inside, like the murmurous swinging of a bell, she heard the answer, 'God, God . . .'.

How long this ineffable moment lasted I never knew. It broke like a bubble at the sudden singing of a bird, and the wind blew and the world was the same as ever – only never *quite* the same.

For her it was not an isolated moment with no before or after but the beginning of a pattern of timeless moments which helped to shape a remarkable life.

The experience so initiated has been the one abiding reality of my life, unalterable except in the abounding fullness and frequency of its occurrence.[3]

Vicars Bell was a little older. Like Willa Muir, he detects an element of 'floating' in his experience of joy. Though it was an isolated moment at eight years old, it left him with an abiding belief in a world of transcendent spiritual reality. What makes his experience interesting and unusual is its introvertive nature. Like some of Wordsworth's experiences, it was 'by form or image unprofaned'.

I think that in my early boyhood my beliefs were something like this. There existed, above the bright blue sky, a Heavenly City. This was a place pervaded by light and music. I was not unaware of its joys, because one night, when I was about eight or so, I retired to bed on my little iron bed-stead in the small, cold, attic bedroom. I put my head on the pillow and closed my eyes. Suddenly, and for a timeless moment, I had an experience of pure joy. In spite of my closed eyes, I was aware that the room was suffused with a warm light. This effluence was in some indescribable way composed of music. The music was formless, beyond comprehension, and not to be retained in memory. But though I could not then, nor can I now, hum or sing it, its essential nature is almost as clear to me now, half a century later, as it was then. There was a sense of levitation, of pure joy such as I have sometimes approached, but never reached since. I have come near to it when confronted by a picture, when listening to or when making music, or when I was timelessly in love.[4]

Richard Jefferies seems to have known an experience which, though starting with the visible, tangible world of nature, soon became similarly devoid of sensuous content. The chronology of events narrated by him in *The Story of My Heart* is difficult to unravel but I estimate he was in his middle teens when every morning he used to watch the sun rise from a secluded spot with a clear view of the East.

> I looked at the hills, at the dewy grass, and then up through the elm branches to the sky. In a moment all that was behind me, the house, the people, the sounds, seemed to disappear, and to leave me alone. Involuntarily I drew a long breath, then I breathed slowly. My thought, or inner consciousness, went up through the illumined sky, and I was lost in a moment of exaltation. This only lasted a very short time, perhaps only part of a second, and while it lasted there was no formulated wish. I was absorbed; I drank the beauty of the morning; I was exalted. When it ceased I did wish for some increase or enlargement of my existence to correspond with the largeness of feeling I had momentarily enjoyed.[5]

There was another kind of experience known to Jefferies, perhaps a more profane one, which he describes as 'feeling myself this moment a hundredfold'. Margiad Evans' moment of joy is of this kind, a sudden euphoric self-consciousness, a spasm of physical well-being.

> I was ten years old. Dressed in a let down, faded, old green cotton dress with feather-stitching round the neck, with bare arms and legs of summer brown and feeling throughout every limb down to the ends of every finger and toe the delight of warmth, youth and unmaterial happiness, standing in a field, and saying to myself, or rather hearing myself say to me: 'This is the best time you'll ever have. Now you are perfect – ten years old.' And never telling any-one, and knowing I was right. As most truly I was.[6]

Margiad Evans was ten years old; she grew up to be one of the most sensitive and least well-known novelists and writers about nature of this century. L. E. Jones was presumably a year or two older. He is describing here what he calls the most memorable moment of his first Summer Half at Eton.

> It is a picture, precise in the sunshine, of Jones minor coming back up Keate's Lane from Lower Chapel on the morning of the Fourth of June. He is wearing a buttonhole; he has just been singing 'Now thank we all our God' with immense and genuine fervour; he is walking in a kind of intoxication. For everything that goes to the making of Eton, the mellow red bricks, the elms, the river and the playing-fields, the traditions, the community, the high privilege of belonging to it, had suddenly coalesced into a single flash of delight. It was a mystic moment for a Thomas Traherne, not for him, to describe. But it left a mark; and I cannot help thinking that a

School which could visit with such a benediction a not very imaginative boy of thirteen must possess a singular grace. At all events it was in Keate's Lane beneath the window-boxes, and not at Harrow, that the vision was vouchsafed.[7]

This kind of experience – much commoner than Vicars Bell's – could be called 'extrovertive' because the 'flash of delight', far from being empty of sensuous content, suddenly trans-figures the world of sense perception. The feeling of well-being and the beauty of the sensible world reflect and complement each other in what Robert Bridges calls 'a superlative brief moment of glory'.

Forrest Reid was about the same age, on the threshold of adolescence, when he responded to the 'rapturous fermen-tation of spring'. The man, recording his childhood with the lost innocence of all post-Freudian autobiographers, is aware of the analogue of sexual stirrings: the boy is conscious only that by stealth he has escaped out of doors from the stifling, comatose piety of a Victorian Sunday afternoon while his mother and aunt doze over their religious books.

> The thick mossy grass was softer than a carpet under my feet. There was a little wind, but not much, and it was warm and scented. There were daffodils, and where the trees were not already clothed with green their branches were covered with buds. The rhododen-drons were covered with buds, too, moist and sticky and bursting with life. Life was everywhere – in the insects, in the birds – colour, joy, ecstasy, music, the mystery of procreation, the mystery of growth and growing things, a kind of intoxication that came with the wind, the scent of flowers and shrubs and grasses, the heat of the sun; and I felt it all thrilling in my own blood as I lifted my head and shook the raindrops down from a dark cedar branch over my face and throat, while my skin tingled deliciously at the wet, cool little touches. It was the rapturous fermentation of spring that I felt, swelling and bursting, piercing up through the brown earth, breaking into flower – breaking into a flame of intense blue that burned and blazed and splashed all over the lush green of the deeper hollows. I drew the air far down into my lungs and raised my voice in my own kind of hymn.[8]

This response to the beauty of the natural world was a natural piety, a 'kind of hymn'. It contained religious feelings of joy, awe and reverence which his religious observances ought to have contained but obviously did not. 'If only I had been asked to worship and to love the earth,' he exclaims, 'I could have done it so easily. If only the earth had been God.'

Forrest Reid's background was the affluent, snobbish, Anglo-Irish middle class: Richard Hillyer's was the servile, forelock-pulling poverty of a farm labourer's tied cottage in a remote Wiltshire village. He left elementary school at the age of fourteen with no prospect but that of following his father and brother in a life-sentence to drudgery on the land of a brutish and irrascible farmer. The future would have looked remorselessly grim were it not that 'a sort of gift for seeing the pleasure in things would break through the misery at times, and drown everything else'.

> Sometimes this pleasure rose, unaccountably, into rapture. Once, I remember, as I was coming home over the rise above the village, the houses below, and the familiar fields, suddenly became incredibly beautiful. They were no different to what they had been before, and yet they were different. Joy burned in them. The sun had set and the trees stood out, sketched with swift black strokes on an orange sky. The great dome of air was swept, and clean. Elation rushed up inside me, as if a barrier had suddenly given way before it. Words, half found lines of poetry, blundered about in my mind, striving to shape themselves into some expression of this intense delight; and in the end verses came, poor, broken-backed things, but seeming at that time to be a miracle.[9]

The small child has no words for the moment of the rose when it comes unless it is the solemn or exalted language learnt in church or chapel. But the adolescent must express what he has felt, be it never so secretly. For Forrest Reid it was a kind of spontaneous hymn; for Richard Hillyer the struggle to create poor blundering verses. It is a pattern which can be found again and again. One of the least controversial things to be said about the experiences recorded in this book is that they lead to a desire, often a feverish intensity, to express the inexpressible.

Most moments are in some measure joyful. In childhood, seemingly, joy may be pure and unalloyed and the telling of it simple, direct and unaccompanied by any penumbra of interpretation or belief. As we grow older it is likely to be tinged with longing or melancholy, awe or fear. It may be the crest of the wave that, of necessity, has its trough as well. Always there is the underlying acuity of the knowledge that the moment is brief and transitory, making

> Ridiculous the waste sad time
> Stretching before and after.

And many share Wordsworth's experience of its loss on the threshold of manhood or, at best, its transmutation into something less sudden, radiant and rare.

Julian Huxley, who has analysed the growth of his own feelings for poetry and natural piety with more than ordinary care, writes of the conflicts that darkened his later adolescence; conflicts between pure lyrical ecstasies of the spirit and the animal passions of sexuality; self-inflicted austerities of life directed towards moral perfection and bursts of work at science: they threatened, he says, to tear his mental being asunder and render him miserable.

> Life would have been intolerable but for glimpses of the alternative state, occasional moments of great happiness and spiritual refreshment, coming usually through poetry or through beautiful landscape, or through people. I had been used, ever since the age of fifteen or sixteen, to have such moments come to me naturally, without effort, in the ordinary course of a full life: and ever since, they had been the things which seemed most valuable in my existence. But now that they were becoming of more vital importance to that life, as assurances that I was not doomed to a miserable existence through having lost the very faculty of experiencing this kind of rapturous or deep joy that permeates and strengthens the mind, they were vouchsafed in diminishing measure, and (although sometimes with very great intensity) more fleetingly. It was no use trying to force these experiences of peace, or reconcilement, or rapture, or those in which supreme value seems within grasp; they came at their sweet will or not at all.[10]

Predictably Huxley speaks of 'shades of the prison house', and in his case it is no hyperbole for they darkened into a serious mental breakdown.

Between high peaks lies the slough of despond; the rose has its thorns and does not grow very far from the yew tree. Margiad, the brown girl in the faded green dress, became an epileptic at the age of forty-two. Each humiliating fit was preceded by feelings of euphoria and heightened awareness: 'The warning symptoms were an emotion by which all things are charged with extra reality and significance,' she says. I wonder whether she knew an undoubtedly autobiographical passage in Dostoievsky's *The Idiot* in which he makes Prince Myshkin say of the moments preceding an epileptic fit: 'These moments, short as they are, when I feel such extreme consciousness of myself and consequently more of life than at other times, are due only to the disease . . . What matter though it be only a dream, an abnormal tension of the brain, if when I recall and analyse the moment, it seems to have been one of harmony and beauty in the highest degree – an instant of deeper sensation, overflowing into unbounded joy and rapture, ecstatic devotion, and completest life?'

The story of Morag Coate, too, should make us cautious travellers in a region full of confusing frontiers.

> I got up from where I had been sitting and moved into another room. Suddenly my whole being was filled with light and loveliness and with an upsurge of deeply moving feeling from within myself to meet and reciprocate the influence that flowed into me. I was in a state of the most vivid awareness and illumination. What can I say of it? A cloudless, cerulean blue sky of the mind, shot through with shafts of exquisite, warm, dazzling sunlight. In its first and most intense stage it lasted perhaps half an hour. It seemed that some force or impulse from without were acting on me, looking into me; that I was in touch with a reality beyond my own; that I had made direct contact with the secret, ultimate source of life. What I had read of the accounts of others acquired suddenly a new meaning. It flashed across my mind, 'This is what the mystics mean by the direct experience of God.'[11]

After six months of frequent and prolonged euphoric experiences of this kind which became increasingly tangled with delusions, she was admitted to a mental hospital seriously ill and diagnosed as schizophrenic. Joy is seldom pure and simple. When St Augustine asks, 'What is that which gleams through me and smites my heart without wounding it? I am both a-shudder and a-glow', it is a real and not a rhetorical question. Am I out of my mind or is this extra-ordinary experience something I must call God?

> My Spirit was awe-stricken with Excess
> And trance-like Depth of its brief Happiness

In these lines from an early version of his ode *Dejection*,

Coleridge pin-points precisely the 'too-muchness', the excess of joy which makes the moment of the rose perplexing, as though it belonged to a dimension other than the one we normally inhabit, one that is strange and a little alarming.

2 *Sudden in a Shaft of Sunlight*

In his Romanes Lecture in 1954 called *Moments of Vision*, Lord Clark said:

> We can all remember those flashes when the object at which we are gazing seems to detach itself from the habitual flux of impressions and becomes intensely clear and important for us. We may not experience these illuminations very often in our busy adult lives, but they were common in our childhood, and given half a chance we could achieve them still. Such moments are the nearest many of us will ever come to the divine agitation of the artist.[1]

Llewelyn Powys was convalescing from an attack of tuberculosis in Switzerland when he had just such an experience of the scene before him seeming to detach itself from the habitual flux of impressions and become intensely clear and important. He was out walking from the sanatorium and, still weak from his long stay in bed, sat down to rest.

> I spent half an hour in front of the mill, seated on a pile of resin-scented pine logs. Presently a peasant leading a mouse-coloured cow, stopped for a drink of red wine. His host came out and stood with him. As I watched them grouped thus before me, so close that I could sometimes feel the moist breath of the animal, I seemed to undergo a kind of mystical revelation as to the reality of concrete life. I became vividly aware of the actual moment, of the cow with its docile, brown eye, of the genial, bearded peasants, of the cup of red, bitter-tasting wine, as if sublimated in some curious way against that eternity of white and blue. Over the snow at my feet a shivering black fly crept, struggling to free each minute hairy foot from the ghastly white waste on which it had settled. I wanted to

24

come to its assistance; but just as I moved, thinking I might persuade it to walk upon my alpenstock, the cow also moved, and an indifferent, cloven hoof carried the persevering insect down into an inch-deep hole of hopeless perdition.[2]

He was 'vividly aware of the actual moment': it was one of those flashes, I suspect, when part of the data of the experience itself is a certainty that it will be indelibly printed on the mind for life. Other examples are gathered in the next chapter. It was also an example of man's capacity for empathy with creatures great and small which links it with the chapter I have called 'Love Beyond Desire'.

Moments of vision are, it seems, not uncommonly associated with illness (particularly tuberculosis) and with convalescence. It may be that the weakness of the body quickens the soul or, perhaps, the confines of the sickroom impose a deprivation of that 'habitual flux of impressions' which makes their resumption more than ordinarily vivid. In either case one is reminded of the self-imposed discipline of some of the acknowledged mystics who mortified the flesh with fasting and flagellation or shut themselves up in caves the better to see the inner light. It may not be an accident, either, as André Gide has pointed out, that of all the Greek city states only Sparta, which liquidated its weakly children, produced no great artists.

The vision may not so much transform the visible world with preternatural vividness; it may rather be of the mind's eye, showing what is not there in truth, a delightful delusion filling, for an instant, the dry concrete pool with water out of sunlight.

I had been ill for some time with a childish complaint. The turning-point had come when I awoke to consciousness one sunny morning after a long refreshing slumber. The sound of soft music broke very pleasantly on my drowsy senses. My brother, in a distant room, was playing an old Welsh air, with a merry lilting iteration, resolving into chords which touched some spring of emotion within me, and I repeated over and over to myself lovingly, like a refrain, the name of the little melody, 'The Bells of Aberdovey'. And at the repetition of these sounds there broke upon my mind's eye the vision of a dewy landscape, fresh as Eden and tremulous with awed anticipation at the opening of a cloudless summer day . . . One flash of glory and it was gone . . .

25

These glimpses of mysteries hinted in flashes so transient and beyond all power to convey their splendours are so closely interwoven with what I suppose were the purely objective experiences of my younger days, that, looked back upon them across the silence of forty years, I seem indeed to have lived in two worlds.[3]

Llewelyn Powys had a vivid revelation of the 'reality of concrete life' and A. F. Webling induced an inward vision by repeating like a chant the name of the old song. Andrew Young, the poet, botanist and clergyman, as a schoolboy had an experience in which the world about him *lost* its substantial, material look and became visionary and dreamlike and he could bring on this state by a reiterated form of words.

> In my boyhood days it was not uncommon for me to have a strange experience. It might happen anywhere, but I remember it best at Dalmeny, when I was playing truant. Suddenly the world around me lost its material look;
>
> > . . . objects of themselves
> > Melted away to their own images,
> > An insubstantial world.
>
> Trees, bushes, fields, rocks, the seashore,
>
> > Nothing was changed, but all was visionary,
> > And I was waking in a dream.
>
> I was looking at a strange world, yet with no sense of surprise. Sometimes I could induce the experience by saying, 'I see what I am seeing', words that suggest it was the world in its true nature I was viewing, or so I felt . . .
>
> With that experience behind me perhaps it was natural I should supplement my theological studies with an interest in mystic writings.[4]

Another poet, Tennyson, from boyhood upwards, frequently induced an ecstatic waking trance by repeating silently his own name, as we shall see in chapter 6. It is not clear what part, if any, these trances played in the genesis or making of his poems but often his moment of vision is the occasion of a writer's first essay in poetic composition. In *Speak, Memory*, Vladimir Nabokov provides an example. He describes an occasion in the summer of 1914 at the age of fifteen when, he says, 'the numb fury of verse-making first came over me'. He had been sheltering alone in a pavilion during a sudden summer thunder-storm followed by sunshine, rainbow and steaming heat.

A moment later my first poem began. What touched it off? I think I know. Without any wind blowing, the sheer weight of a raindrop, shining in parasitic luxury on a cordate leaf, caused its tip to dip, and what looked like a globule of quicksilver performed a sudden glissando down the centre vein, and then having shed its bright load, the relieved leaf unbent. Tip, leaf, dip, relief – the instant it all took to happen seemed to me not so much a fraction of time as a fissure in it, a missed heartbeat, which was refunded at once by a patter of rhymes: I say 'patter' intentionally, for when a gust of wind did come, the trees would briskly start to drip all together in as crude an imitation of the recent downpour as the stanza I was already muttering resembled the spasm of wonder I had experienced when for a moment heart and leaf had been one.[5]

It was a moment out of time and also one of union when 'heart and leaf had been one'.

A. L. Rowse, the historian and poet, was a little older, sixteen or seventeen, when he wrote his first poem and the moment that occasioned it came to him again alone and equally suddenly, but in a shaft of moonlight or starlight.

Once when I was coming home from choir-practice – as usual alone, for my brother and earlier companions had grown up and gone – I was overcome by, I was possessed by, the beauty of the night. It was the very beginning of March 1920; it was frosty and the sky was alive with stars. I must often have noticed starlight and moonlight before; indeed I remember still, occasions from my childhood when I noticed them, the stars flung out over the hill-side that bounded our view to the north, the moon bathing the fields below the village with a soft misty glow, or lighting up the bay with path-ways of silver. But never had I noticed before with such intensity; the sensation of being possessed was a physical one: I *was* 'possessed'. In spite of there being a bright moon the stars shone clear like jewels; I saw them entangled among the wintry branches of the hedgerow, as I came up the last bend of the road by the farm before entering the village. I noticed that in spite of the clear, glittering brilliance, there was colour in the sky: it was frost-blue.

I hurried home, my mind on fire, went straight to bed to be by myself and think of nothing but writing my poem . . . Years later, I can say that it was the fact of writing the poem which fixed that night for ever in my mind.[6]

This was not an isolated act of creation but the beginning

27

of a life-long habit which was more like a religious observance than the hobby of a scholar; it 'absorbed the most intimate impulses of my emotional life,' he says.

There are other unforgettable moments recorded in Rowse's book which gave him 'an unease of heart, some reaching out towards perfection such as impels men into religion, some sense of the transcendence of things.' For him they were not *unattended* moments: his careful account of how he laboured to understand them and how they influenced his subsequent beliefs is full and exceptionally interesting Some writers have found in their ecstatic experiences a triumphant assurance of a spiritual immortality transcending mortal death. For Rowse they speak of transcience and the acute piognancy of the moment lies in the knowledge that it *is* momentary and time moves inexorably on.

We will return to Rowse's *A Cornish Childhood* once more in the next chapter but end this one with a passage from another Cornish writer, Sir Arthur Quiller-Couch.

I am sure that the beauty of Bradley Woods had insensibly haunted me for a year or two; since, without knowing why, I had so often made for them and solitude. But that afternoon, as I leant on the rail of a footbridge . . . I happened to glance up on my right and was met by a vision. 'Twas of nothing more (reduced to simplest terms) than sunlight slanting down a broad glade between two woodlands that drowsed in the summer heat. But it held me at gaze while the mere beauty of it flooded into my veins, and the mysterious bliss of it shook my young body. Also, when I came to recall the scene, a deep silence held it: the water slid without noise under the footboards, no note of bird broke the afternoon hush. But this may have been a later fancy.

The reader may smile, thinking that I make too much of a very trivial experience: but, after all, this is my book and must record experiences on the scale of their importance to my own life.

Up to that moment I dare say the beauty of the world about me had been as pleasant to me as to most boys – . . . This, however, was, if not a revelation, at least a wandering surmise, almost an assurance, of a beauty behind all phenomena; active through them, immanent, beneficent.

I believe, looking back, that this apprehension finally chased away those religious terrors which had beset me so miserably. Anyhow, it has companioned me to this day, even through evil times. *He maketh me to lie down in green pastures: he leadeth me beside the still waters.* Visions thus penetrating have their reaction, certainly for one doomed to be a writer, in an ache to express the inexpressible.[7]

This flash of collusion with beauty was literally 'sudden in a shaft of sunlight' and the radiance of it both dispelled the religious nightmares of an imaginative child and lighted the path of a prolific and versatile writer, a conjunction of consequences which we have seen before and will see again.

3 Echoes in the Memory

About experiences, William James says, 'Of some, no memory survives the instant of their passage. Of others, it is confined to a few moments, hours or days. Others again, leave vestiges which are indestructible, and by means of which they may be recalled as long as life endures.'[1] The more modern theory is that every experience from pre-natal days onwards is stored electro-chemically in the brain's computer and could, in theory, be recalled if we knew the right button to press. Forgetting is not a wiping clean of the slate but a filing away in a system which we only partly comprehend and over which we have only a little conscious control. We forget what we do not use, what we do not need and, as Freud showed, what we do not want to remember. But William James was certainly right in the sense that some experiences, and not necessarily ones which are remarkable in themselves, seem to imprint themselves more deeply and vividly than others on the filing-cards of memory and when we recall them, or when they come back seemingly of their own volition, they can have a vividness of sight, sound, touch, taste and smell which is no pale reflection only of the original experience. What is it that impresses some experiences so firmly? Often we cannot tell and certainly it is dangerous to generalize but usually the answer seems to be the pressure of powerful emotions.

In her study of involuntary memories called *A Collection of Moments*,[2] Esther Salaman develops the theory that vivid involuntary memories which she calls 'precious fragments' are always associated with events containing some element of shock or disturbance which the mind has forgotten or suppressed. At any rate, strong feelings seem to produce vivid memories and vivid memories may bring back something of the feeling that accompanied the original experience.

When we read memoirs, we cannot always know for sure, unless the author tells us, which, if any, of the recollected scenes and events of his life are memories with the peculiar vividness of unattended moments. But usually there are clues:

> And one other walk, that I hope in my last hour to remember; it was in cold February, and we walked far over the downs, over the white dead grass, dry and crisp in the wind; and we rested a little and ate in a place where a little mound rose above the hill. And we watched, in the valley beneath us, tiny children running to school beside a little blue trickle of water, and large gulls were washing and flapping their wings in the water. The children called to them and waved their arms, and the gulls rose and spread like snow-flakes over the valley, and the children ran on holding each other's hands and singing.[3]

The fact that T. F. Powys hoped (and, I think, expected) this moment to remain with him till his dying hour suggests that it was indeed a moment of vision and of joy. It stands out concrete and compelling from a context of misty generalities and prophetic rumblings in his *Soliloquies of a Hermit* which hardly add up to an autobiography in the ordinary sense. He describes the scene with a clarity and economy of language, in fact with an artistry, that suggests his mind and feelings were more than ordinarily engaged by what he saw and the memory of it, and something of the quality of the experience is conveyed to the reader. This is, perhaps, a part of the meaning of the complex notion 'inspiration'.

What is it that makes these 'unfading recollections' come rushing back into the mind? Sometimes they come

In vacant or in pensive mood

flooding in, as it were, to fill a vacuum. But they may equally well come elbowing their way into a mind already pre-occupied with present business. Often there is no clue as to why they return. But sometimes the signal that calls them forth is plain enough. For Proust it was the taste of the *petite madeleine* 'moulded in the fluted scallop of a pilgrim's shell' and dipped in a spoonful of tea which suddenly unlocked memories of his childhood at Combray. For Cowper writing *The Task* it was the sound of the village chimes:

> With easy force it opens all the cells
> Where mem'ry slept.

For many people smells are more potent than taste or sound. With Margiad Evans it was the missing page of an old bird book that made the bright images return. This is from a section of her autobiography called 'Journals at Dawn'.

13th March and no buds yet. How winter has leant on the land. From the hilltops you can see miles and miles of pale country: in the hedges grasses dead and withered, slack bracken, gaps and broken places, and yet green grass springing in the banks, like corn sprouting in an old basket. Plovers and rooks fly high: the nests are flattened, the thorns like dead rubbish. I went to bed early and read the old bird book which was my godmother's in 1866. It is of faded purple and gilt binding, with coloured plates of stone eggs suspended in space. The page on Yellow Hammers was gone. Yellow Hammers to me will always mean a walk with grandfather and myself rushing from bush to bush in shocks of anticipation un-ashamed by the calm figure in a black coat strolling behind me. I can still see through the lifeless medium of this stolid print the light that flashed from the flint stones on the field, their dark blueness, like thick glass where they were chipped, the seedling green of the corn they could not prevent, the sunlight, the yellow soil and the long brambles dipping into the grass. Oh exquisite, uncom-municable time! I was eleven years old then, on that day, my vision began. It lapsed: it failed, but it always came again, re-newing my being, filling my breast like a fountain, opening my eyes. Lying on my bed not only do the bright images return, but their meaning and sum, the growing universe around the sun, its worship, its beauty, its glorious loneliness. That day was marked: sight began and I began, for the first time, to see that there was a Life which was not mine. 'There is something out of doors.' I said that to myself, but I could never bring my life to utter the words aloud. They sounded in my inmost being, clear, emphatic, in-explicable. I thought the wind was a god – there was to me such

31

holiness . . . My blood flushes to the skin and my heart is *freed* by the memories of those first joyous pains! [4]

There was nothing fragmentary or arbitrary about this memory, it seems, for it was of a day marked as the beginning of her visions and intimate communion with that 'something out of doors' which, in his 'Lines written above Tintern Abbey', Wordsworth called 'A presence that disturbs me with the joy Of elevated thoughts'. It is right that Wordsworth should be remembered here, for not only was his *Prelude*, after Rousseau's *Confessions*, one of the first great autobiographies; not only was he the first great writer properly to value and describe moments of vision, 'spots of time'; but the very essence of his poetry was 'emotion recollected in tranquillity' and it was the mountains, lakes and clouds of his native country at all seasons and in all weathers that were a main source of that emotion.

Memory can be fickle, as we all know to our cost. We can summon past scenes and events like spirits from the vasty deep but they will not always come when we call them. Today we take photographs or buy postcards as souvenirs: in Wordsworth's day one had to make sketches or employ a landscape artist. When he first visited the Alps as a young man on a walking tour with his college friend Robert Jones, he had no talent for sketching and no money to buy etchings or paintings: there was nothing grand about their tour. He was constantly in a fever of anxiety that he would not be able to retain the magnificent scenery through which they passed. He wrote to his sister Dorothy,

Ten thousand times in the course of this tour have I regretted the inability of my memory to retain a more strong impression of the beautiful forms before me; and again and again in quitting a fortunate station, have I returned to it with the most eager avidity, in the hope of bearing away a more lively picture.

Perhaps scenes like these need to be laid down in the vaults of the memory for a while before they can be brought up and decanted. At least, Wordsworth need not have doubted the vividness of the memories that would subsequently be 'the bliss of solitude'. As the years passed, he learnt to trust his memory and when some eight years later he looked down on the River Wye from just such another 'fortunate station' a few miles above Tintern Abbey he knew that

> in this moment there is life and food
> For future years.

The metaphor of laying down wines is not a bad one for those vintage moments since, judging by the number of fine autobiographies of childhood which have been written in old age, they seem to improve with keeping. When Wittgenstein, the great philosopher, was told that Esther Salaman was writing memories of her childhood he said, 'I'm much older than she, but I couldn't do it yet.' It was a wise remark. Memories of our younger days do not simply fade away like water-colours exposed to sunlight. Perhaps the old have the leisure and the patience to recollect the past that we lack in our more active years or perhaps it is that as we grow old and infirm we like best to remember ourselves at our freest, happiest, least burdened or impaired.

I said in the last chapter that I thought part of the basic data of some rare moments was the certainty that, without any of Wordsworth's anxious effort among the Alps, one would always be able to recall them in all their original clarity. We can return to Margiad Evans' *Autobiography* for a vivid example:

I am twelve years old, reading on the window sill in the fruit shed. I am kneeling on a wicker hamper, and my knees are numb. The daylight is cold and cramped. Rubbing my hands I sniff the air. The hamper is full of old newspapers and the atmosphere tastes of them and of pearskins and mouldy portmanteaux.

I have read myself out of existence. No such person inhabits the dark day; but suddenly I come awake with a rush of feeling. My crowded head feels suddenly clear, empty and airy as craning out of the window, I look hungrily around. This is real, I think, the colours, the brick, the ivy. It is as though something is going to be shown to me, once and for ever. Things seem so *clear*; they seem to declare themselves aloud. My eyes have touch, my skin on which the air plays seems to be as glass through which I can look from every pore. Awake, awake to all, I know it is a rare moment, perhaps a beginning of a life separate from ordinary existence.

And yet what is there? The elm tree dropping leaves yellow golden all over, into the rainwater tank. They slide slowly downward on the point and settle with the faintest breath of sound on the olive surface. And below them, in the cube of water, like things tranced in ice are others suspended on edge and rotting. Then there is the pipe, and the gray cobwebs stretched across the corners of the tank, and then suddenly the bright shadow of the tree itself with all its stars of sky – lovely but gone almost before it can be lovely.

I lean out, sighing with the strange feeling in me. I can touch the cold sides of the tank; I feel as though I can touch with my mind the tree trunk, the hedge, the hurdle, even the farthest hill that I can see. What are all these familiar things saying so clearly? Why have I never seen them like this before? A moment ago they existed but quietly and without me. Now the leaves keep falling so queerly – queerly as though I had something to do with their falling. Something is happening which makes me able to say and know that it is true: 'I shall remember this. I shall remember each vein on each leaf. I shall be able to see this whenever I want to, wherever I am!'[5]

By contrast, with some 'spots of time', it is only when the memory persistently and involuntarily returns to them that they are known for what they are, imperishable. Thus it was with Basil Willey.

We were dissatisfied with our boarding-house at Ilfracombe, and disliked the noise and crowds there; so one morning we took the train to Morthoe station, alighting there for the two mile walk down to Woolacombe Bay. It was a perfect summer morning, and at that little country station (as it was then) there was no one else about. As we emerged into the sunshine, the solitude and the stillness and the warmth sank into our hearts like a benediction, and a bed of August flowers – asters and zinnias – glowed in the bright, seaside air with a preternatural brilliance. My spirits bounded up, and I cared no more about the rest of the day: I had had my reward. Woolacombe was delightful, but what mattered was that peace could be as deep, silence as complete, and flowers as bright, as they were that morning outside Morthoe station. Naturally, I did not know this at the time; my conscious mind was still bent upon the picnic at the Bay, and I little thought that what would remain with me all my life was that visionary moment. So it often is: the unregarded thing is what enters the mind's recesses, while the conscious preoccupations leave not a wrack behind.[6]

These visionary moments, unfading recollections, may return involuntarily or sometimes, in 'sessions of sweet silent thought', we may deliberately 'summon up remembrance of things past'. This has been the habit of A. L. Rowse, who is here writing about himself at the age of three or four.

It was a still evening in early summer, for the bluebells were out in Doctor's fields up on the hill-side. And it was a Sunday evening, for we were all walking in the fields together, a very rare event: I never remember it happening again. As we walked, we picked bluebells in the cool of the evening. And then from far over the shoulder of the hill-side to the west there came the silvery sound of the bells of St Mewan ringing to church, so rare a sound, so far away, we very rarely heard them, like church-bells in a dream on a May morning. The thought of those bells brings tears to my eyes; their memory speaks to me of my buried childhood, brings back that moment in the cool evening, the bluebells gathered, the thorn hedges in leaf, father and mother and the children that we were for once at one, my father now dead, all of us scattered, the unity broken . . .

When I think of my life as a whole, I do not in the end think of myself, but of the sum of those moments of ecstasy which is my real inner life.[7]

The last example will conclude this chapter and also form a bridge to the next. It is another of those memories of early childhood recalled with great vividness in old age. Margaret Isherwood had the experience when she was nine years old but only 'possessed' it nearly a lifetime later.

On one quiet Sunday afternoon at the age of nine I carried a baby sister down the sandy lane to the bottom of the garden. Crossing the stream by the stepping stones, I laid her down under some sweet-smelling lime trees which were in bloom. Everything was very quiet save for the bubbling water and the lazy munching of the melancholy cows. I was not thinking of anything in particular but I must have absorbed the total ambience very deeply for after nearly seventy years it is all still quite clear and still 'holy ground'.

The 'Thing' happened suddenly but quietly as if I had been wakened from a dream. It is well known that we have no language in which to describe the experience of the numenal.

> To those who know Thee not, no words can paint
> And those who know Thee know all words are faint.

So, like the prophet Ezekiel, I must fall back on symbolic terms and say 'The Heavens were opened' or 'It was as if a veil had been drawn and I saw a far country', which was not 'far' but all around, filling me with wonder and gladness.

I remember saying 'Now I know what heaven is like.' Then I found myself repeating the twenty-third Psalm . . .[8]

The experience was instantly associated by the little girl with the idea of heaven and with familiar passages of biblical poetry. Despite this it was then totally forgotten until the memory came back suddenly as a relevant 'fact of experience' in the adult's prolonged and painful search for a religious faith. It was seen as belonging to a pattern of timeless moments in which religious and aesthetic strands were inextricably woven together. What reason alone was inadequate to provide, 'facts of experience' like these remembered moments helped to secure. They were, she says, more important than anything she learnt from books and lectures in her search for meaning.

4 *The Impossible Union*

Ecstasy, in the strict theological sense, is a state of being 'beside' (or outside) oneself in which the soul leaving the body temporarily is united with God. To call any state of rapturous happiness 'ecstatic', as some of the writers already quoted do, is an accepted hyperbole. Similarly, when the soul is united with God, that experience and that alone is properly called 'mystical', though loosely we may call 'mystical' that feeling of being united with something other than ourselves such as Nature or the universe. Robert Bridges chooses his words carefully when he writes of

> that mystic rapture, the consummation of which
> is the absorption of Selfhood in the Being of God.

Mystical is an even more slippery word than ecstasy, though; starting with 'mist' it ends in schism, as some wag has remarked. As William James warns, it may be used 'as a term of mere reproach, to throw at any opinion which we regard as vague and vast and sentimental, and without a base in either fact or logic'.[1]

The first example in this chapter is, perhaps, a border-line case, hovering on the threshold of ecstasy and the mystical.

Osbert Sitwell was only five years old and staying at the seaside – presumably Scarborough which old Sir George thought salubrious. It had been one of those days of temper tantrums and punishment and when they went out in the evening, all passions spent, Osbert slipped quietly away from nurse Davis.

I ran to the edge of the precipitous cliff and stood there looking straight in the face of the evening sun. The light bathed the whole world in its amber and golden rays, seeming to link up every object and every living thing, catching them in its warm diaphanous net, so that I felt myself at one with my surroundings, part of the same boundless immensity of sea and sky and, even, of the detailed precision of the landscape, part of the general creation, divided from it by no barriers made by man or devil. Below me and above me stretched the enormous merging of blue air and blue water with golden air and golden water, fathomless, and yet more and more fervently glowing every moment, the light revealing new vistas and avenues up into space or out towards the horizon, as though the illimitable future itself opened for me, and, as I watched, I lost myself . . . All this must have endured only an instant, for presently – but time had ceased to exist – I heard Davis calling. The eye of the sun was lower now. The clouds began to take on a deeper and more rosy hue, and it was time for me to return home: but this strange peace, of which poetry is born, had for the first time descended on me and henceforth a new light quivered above the world and over the people in it. Like Cellini before me, I had seen the Salamander.[2]

He lost himself for an instant, he felt himself at one with his surroundings but he calls it 'my first Dionysian or rhapsodic experience' and, once again, it is associated with the springs of art rather than religion. The Salamander in the flames is the symbol of art.

Most of the other examples quoted in this chapter are descriptions of what the theologian would call the humble 'nature-mystical' type of union, though it is a nice question (which I shall leave an open one) whether the experience of the nature-mystic is essentially different from what the acknowledged religious mystic feels, except, of course, in the interpretation he puts upon it.

We have already seen Willa Muir at the age of two experiencing for the first time what she calls a nameless 'floating' experience and an uprush of joyousness. It recurred from time to time:

> One evening when I was sixteen it broke over me so strongly and lasted so long that I was awed into giving it a name.
>
> I was sitting alone in a boat beached at the back of the island in the throat of the tidal lagoon, called the Basin, behind Montrose; the sun was setting before me and the Basin was full. Except for a distant curlew's call there was no living sound. The feeling came upon me like a tide floating me out and up into the wide greening sky – into the Universe, I told myself. That was the secret name I gave it: Belonging to the Universe. Like Thoreau, I felt myself 'grandly related'.[3]

She says that this experience 'was of great and secret importance in my life' and the recognition that Edwin Muir knew and cherished some similar experience, she suggests, was one of the factors that drew them together. However, Edwin Muir's own excellent autobiography contains no explicit corroboration.

We have also already quoted Forrest Reid who, as a small child, knew a 'consoling feeling of fellowship' with nature and could have worshipped the earth so much more easily than the God presented to him by the mentors of his pious upbringing. In his teens he developed a kind of personal animism coloured by his reading of the Greek legends.

> A mysterious and deep understanding, it seemed to me, had existed in that far-off age between man and nature, and this understanding I shared today, or thought I shared. There were hours when I could pass *into* nature, and feel the grass growing, and float with the clouds through the transparent air; when I could hear the low breathing of the earth, when the colour and the smell of it were so close to me that I seemed to lose consciousness of any separate existence. Then, one single emotion animated all things, one heart beat throughout the universe, and the mother and all her children were united . . .[4]

How very common (and yet, paradoxically, how rare and precious) is this feeling of being grandly related, of belonging to the universe, indeed of being absorbed into its life. Here is Margiad Evans again:

> Sometimes I seem to know each separate thing while lost in the one, and then it is that I feel profoundly the almost palpable linking up

of the universe. From life to life, from kind to kind, through the mind to the sky and out to each planet, the chain reaches. Ah, who can doubt it? Who that really feels what he sees can fail to be sure, if he thinks at all of what his senses tell him? The air itself is felt to be woven of threads of life. Even in the darkness they are there.

So common and yet so elusive and transitory, it is little wonder the moment is often unattended.

Ah, how impossible it is to keep those moments, to hold down for more than a single instant that joy of being oneself contained in all one sees![5]

A normally unemphatic writer is forced by the experience to resort to exclamations, metaphor, and repeated rhetorical questions.

Nearly always it is an instant, a second, a flash, a moment out of time. Vladimir Nabokov recounts a butterfly-hunting expedition to a marsh near his native St Petersburg on a hot June day and then adds:

I confess I do not believe in time. I like to fold my magic carpet, after use, in such a way as to superimpose one part of the pattern upon another. Let visitors trip. And the highest enjoyment of timelessness – in a landscape selected at random – is when I stand among rare butterflies and their food plants. This is ecstasy, and behind the ecstasy is something else, which is hard to explain. It is like a momentary vacuum into which rushes all that I love. A sense of oneness with sun and stone. A thrill of gratitude to whom it may concern – to the contrapuntal genius of human fate or to tender ghosts humouring a lucky mortal.[6]

Writer after writer struggles to put into words that mysterious sense of oneness with sun and stone half afraid, as Emerson says, that 'Everyman's words, who speaks from that life, must sound vain to those who do not dwell in the same thought on their own part.' Here is Edward Carpenter.

The sense is a sense that one *is* those objects and things and persons that one perceives, (and even that one is the whole universe), – a sense in which sight and touch and hearing are all fused in identity. Nor can the matter be understood without realising that the whole faculty is deeply and intimately rooted on the far side of the moral and emotional nature, and beyond the thought region of the brain.[7]

And here is John Cowper Powys, the third brother of the

family we have quoted, writing about himself as a young man at Cambridge.

> My grand object was to get off for lonely walks in the country. All my life I have been like this. I have always regarded my existing domicile . . . as a resting-place from which I could walk *into the country* . . . What I am revealing to you now is the deepest and most essential secret of my life. My thoughts were lost in my sensations; and my sensations were of a kind so difficult to describe that I could write a volume upon them and still not really have put them down . . .
>
> A mysterious satisfaction . . . seemed to well up from the inner being of old posts, old heaps of stone, old haystacks thatched with straw . . . What I should like to emphasise just here is that the pleasure I got from these things of my solitary walks did not present itself to me as an *aesthetic* pleasure, nor did it call up in my mind the idea of beauty. What gave me these sensations seemed to be some mysterious 'rapport' between myself and these things. It was like a sudden recognition of some obscure link, some remote identity, between myself and these objects. Posts, palings, hedges, heaps of stones – they were part of my very soul.[8]

For him the highest happiness, the greatest good lay in those moments when communion or rapport deepened into a feeling of absorbing or being absorbed by the universe but one suspects that people who share to some extent his creed, like Richard Jefferies and Margiad Evans, despite their stress on moments of joy, are dark, passionate, turbulent spirits much preoccupied with thoughts of death and dissolution.

Although John Cowper Powys says his feeling was not aesthetic it is interesting, but not particularly surprising, to find that some painters share with poets and writers that mysterious rapport with the 'furniture of earth'. Sir William Rothenstein wrote in his recollections, *Men and Memories*,[9] that 'one's very being seems to be absorbed into the fields, trees and the walls one is striving to paint' and believed the experience of painting out of doors gave him insight into the poetry of the great mystics, European and Eastern. 'At rare moments while painting,' he says, 'I have felt myself caught, as it were, in a kind of cosmic rhythm; but such experiences are usually all too brief.' Ben Nicholson is, perhaps, saying the same thing more laconically when he is quoted in a monograph on his work as remarking, 'As I see it, painting and religious experience are the same thing,' and Lord Clark, in a lecture we have already quoted from, sums up the matter in the following words:

> The child, the ordinary man, and the creative artist are all moved by a flash of self-identification in the same way, but there is no doubt that the child is moved more often and that these flashes illuminate his whole being with a more penetrating light . . . it is questionable if there is any central image in an artist's work which did not come to him as a moment of vision in childhood.[10]

The feeling of being caught up in the rhythm of the universe and absorbed into the fields and trees and animal life of nature is sometimes wrongly called 'pantheistic'. Strictly pantheism (all-God-ism) is the doctrine that the whole universe is God and that there is no God apart from the forces and laws of the universe. As such it has been severely censured by the church through the ages for it cannot be reconciled with the Christian notion of a personal God and transcendent Creator. The experience described by most of the writers in this chapter is more properly called 'panenhenic' (all-in-one).

Martin Buber, the great Austro-Jewish theologian, is careful to distinguish a variety of unattended moments which he knew in his youth and may then have thought of as 're-ligious' from the aweful claim to have had an experience of God.

> In my earlier years the 'religious' was for me the exception. There were hours that were taken out of the course of things. From some-where or other the firm crust of everyday was pierced. Then the reliable permanence of appearances broke down; the attack which took place burst its law asunder. 'Religious experience' was the experience of an otherness which did not fit into the context of life. It could begin with something customary, with consideration of some familiar object, but which then became unexpectedly mysterious and uncanny, finally lighting a way into the lightning-pierced darkness of the mystery itself. But also, without any inter-mediate stage, time could be torn apart – first the firm world's structure then the still firmer self-assurance flew apart and you were delivered to fulness. The 'religious' lifted you out. Over there now lay the accustomed existence with its affairs, but here illumination and ecstasy and rapture held, without time or sequence. Thus your own being encompassed a life here and a life beyond, and there was no bond but the actual moment of the transition.

Now from my own unforgettable experience I know well that there is a state in which the bonds of the personal nature of life seem to have fallen away from us and we experience an undivided unity. But I do not know – what the soul willingly imagines and indeed is bound to imagine (mine too once did it) – that in this I had attained to a union with the primal being or the godhead. That is an exaggeration no longer permitted to the responsible understanding. Responsibly – that is, as a man holding his ground before reality – I can elicit from those experiences only that in them I reached an undifferentiable unity of myself without form or content.[11]

This is the cautious theologian writing but it is not difficult to see how many mystics and poets like Wordsworth and Goethe who had powerful experiences of this 'undivided unity' should be suspected of pantheism. Wordsworth is recorded as having said:

In childhood . . . I was often unable to think of external things as having external existence, and I communed with all that I saw as something not apart from, but inherent in, my own immaterial nature. Many times while going to school have I grasped at a wall or tree to recall myself from this abyss of idealism to the reality. At that time I was afraid of such processes.[12]

As a young man he occasionally gave expression to explicitly pantheistic views:

the one interior life . . .
In which all beings live with God, themselves
Are God, existing in the mighty whole,
As indistinguishable as the cloudless East
Is from the cloudless West, when all
The hemisphere is one cerulean blue.

But this was an unpublished fragment of verse discovered by his great editor, Ernest de Selincourt. Wordsworth was generally cautious, particularly in later life, to tone down any passages which might give offence to the orthodox: he even omitted from the final version of *The Prelude* the lines in which earlier he had described his happy seventeenth year:

In all things now
I saw one life and felt that it was joy.

Remembering the age of seventeen, Julian Huxley very clearly associates the beginning of his love life with first attempts at writing poetry, with ecstatic moments of collusion with beauty and with experience of impossible union in which he 'became the universe'.

My love life coincided with the onset of my desire to write poetry, and that began on manoeuvres on Salisbury Plain, when I was just seventeen. On the great flat expanse, one summer evening, I was seized with an oceanic feeling and wrote my first poem, in which the words 'away to the farthest horizon' recurred at the end of each stanza. It wasn't a very good poem, but it started me on a mild career – the excitement of actually creating a poem of my own was overwhelming . . .

As I write these pages, other memories of Eton, disconnected and often trivial, surge up. Between obvious growing pains and the stress of constant new adjustments I remember a clear night when, coming back from my tutor's, I found myself alone in School Yard. Lying between two buttresses of Chapel, I looked at the stars and felt I could in some way *possess* even their immensity. The joy of it filled my heart like a revelation, a reassurance that the world of natural beauty meant something important to me, and to the world. Another peaceful and penetrating glimpse of what I may call nature's poetry came on College Field when, waiting my turn to bat, I stalked off towards the arches spanning a brook. There I saw the pure blue of the wild meadow geranium in the lush grass – an unforgettable discovery of beauty in a common plant.

These moments, when I felt mystically united with nature, were very precious. The most extraordinary came to me at a dance at Shackleford. Wandering out into the fragrant night air, the sky crowded with stars, I had a strange cosmic vision – as if I could *see* right down into the centre of the earth, and embrace the whole of its contents and its animal and plant inhabitants. For a moment I *became*, in some transcendental way, the universe.[13]

Finally in this chapter here are two passages which will form a bridge with that 'Love Beyond Desire' which is the subject of the next. The first is from Richard Hillyer, whose unattended moments were the one consolation for his cheerless lot as a fifteen-year-old farm labourer. Poems could touch them off – as, no doubt, would music have done had there been any music in his life – and so could sun and stone, bird or twig and even, sometimes, people.

Those sudden exaltations that exploded around me, out of nowhere, were what I had to hang on to at all costs; and yet I could not hang on to them, for they came and went as they pleased. Sometimes it was a poem, or a piece of prose, that touched off the magic, that

43

brought the lift of the heart that was like a fountain breaking into
the sunlight. Sometimes just an ordinary thing would suddenly
make itself new and marvellous . . . Then everything quickened,
and there was a feeling of unity with all the world, and mysteries
made clear. It might happen with people sometimes, though not to
the same extent. Suppose I happen to be walking up Brandy Hole
Lane, on a summer evening, and see a fat girl painting a garden
gate. Nothing extraordinary, just that. She is bending at the knees
a little, to get down to it, so she bulges in different places. Suddenly
I know what she feels like, laying that paint on thick, and black,
watching it settle down into a smooth coat, with an enjoyment that
is almost sensual; and adding to the pleasure by thinking, at the
same time, about what she is going to have for supper. But moments
like this could not be forced, they came of themselves or not at all.[14]

Richard Hillyer could feel what it was like to be the fat girl
painting the gate. John Stuart Mill called imagination this
'power by which one human being enters into the mind and
circumstances of another', and Wordsworth thought it 'the
mightiest lever known to the moral world'. He came to believe that the moments of self-obliterating love of nature he
had known had led him to love man and to hear the still sad
music of humanity. We can call this power of entering into
the mind and circumstances of another person imagination
or empathy or sympathy or morality indifferently, for the
impossible union, like all unattended moments, goes beyond
the reach of ordinary words.

One last example comes from Jacquetta Hawkes. On a
moonlight night in Palestine she wandered a little distance from
the camp and was suddenly possessed by an immense exaltation and sense of illumination.

So powerfully was I moved by this sense of possession that I climbed
up on to a high outcrop of rock against the mouth of the wadi and
knelt down there. The moonlight swam round, and in, my head as
I knelt looking across the plain to the shining silver bar of the
Mediterranean.

From far behind me, still muffled in the folds of the mountain, I
heard the bronze sound of camel-bells. To my sharpened but
converging senses they seemed like a row of brown flowers blooming
in the moonlight. In truth the sound of bells came from nothing
more remarkable than a caravan, perhaps twenty camels with
packs and riders, coming down the wadi on its way north to Haifa.
But even now I cannot recognise that caravan in such everyday

terms; my memory of it is dreamlike, yet embodies one of the most intense sensuous and emotional experiences of my life . . .

I found myself comprehending every physical fact of their passage as though it were a part of my own existence. I knew how the big soft feet of the camels pressed down upon and embraced the rough stones of the path; I knew the warm depth of their fur and the friction upon it of leather harness and the legs of the riders; I knew the blood flowing through the bodies of men and beasts and thought of it as echoing the life of the anemones which now showed black among the rocks around me . . .

So the swaying line came from behind, went past, and moved away across the plain. It was a procession of life moving through the icy moonlight. It was coming from the mountains and going towards the sea. That was all I knew, but as the moon leapt and bounded in the sky I took full possession of a love and confidence that have not yet forsaken me.[15]

5 Love Beyond Desire

In a letter to his friend Bailey dated 22 November 1817 Keats wrote:

The setting Sun will always set me to rights – or if a Sparrow come before my Window I take part in its existence and pick about the Gravel.

The quotations in this chapter will suggest that there is a mysterious connection between the sort of 'feeling good' that can irradiate the heart from the light of setting suns, and being and doing good in a moral sense. A love of sunsets, flowers or poetry is not an *infallible* sign of moral sensibility: life is not, alas, as simple as that. The phrase 'feeling good' may be anathema to the moral philosopher but then, as T. S. Eliot says, what we are talking about is

. . . not the sense of well-being,
Fruition, fulfilment, security or affection,
Or even a very good dinner, but the sudden illumination – [1]

45

The connection between sudden illumination and our capacity to love our neighbours is not a mere whimsical opinion like Coleridge's belief that a man who refuses apple dumplings cannot have a pure mind, though both may be irrational. Similarly, the connection between imaginative capacity to identify oneself with a sparrow picking about the gravel and to respond in a moral way to one's fellow human beings is a matter of the heart's reasons as much as logic. 'Response' is the important word and moral responsibility is a matter of *responding* with the heart as much as the head. Keats' contemporary, Shelley, in his *Defence of Poetry* put it like this:

A man to be greatly good, must imagine intensely and comprehensively; he must put himself in the place of another and of many others; the pains and pleasures of his species must become his own.

In the last chapter we have seen Richard Hillyer's imaginative self-identification with the fat girl painting the gate and thinking about her supper and Jacquetta Hawkes' loving and intimate comprehension of the life of rider and camel as the caravan passed down towards the sea. About that moonlight encounter she has written:

. . . my memory of it is dreamlike, yet embodies one of the most intense sensuous and emotional experiences of my life. For those minutes, and I have no notion how many they were, I had the heightened sensibility of one passionately in love and with it the power to transmute all that the senses perceived into symbols of burning significance. This surely is one of the best rewards of humanity. To be filled with comprehension of the beauty and marvellous complexity of the physical world, and for this happy excitement of the senses to lead directly into an awareness of spiritual significance. The fact that such experience comes most surely with love, with possession by the creative eros, suggests that it belongs near the root of our mystery. Certainly it grants man a state of mind in which I believe he must come more and more to live: a mood of intensely conscious individuality which serves only to strengthen an intense consciousness of unity with all being. His mind is one infinitesimal node in the mind present throughout all being, just as his body shares in the unity of matter.[2]

This, it will be noticed, is an entirely secular, not to say pagan, account of what might be thought a profoundly religious experience. It is not difficult to imagine how another writer with a different set of beliefs would feel compelled to invoke notions like grace, beatitude, the Holy Spirit and divine love in describing such an experience rather than 'heightened sensibility' and 'creative eros'. Indeed, Jacquetta Hawkes uses the word 'spiritual' without, one suspects, intending to imply belief in a non-physical reality. This is often a problem, for our language is so saturated with our Christian cultural heritage that it is not always possible to tell whether a writer wants his words to be understood literally or metaphorically. Sometimes he may not know himself.

Here is another equally 'secular' account of an experience which may perhaps have been less powerful and more transitory than Jacquetta Hawkes'. Cecil Day Lewis was about eighteen, nearing the end of his schooldays at Sherborne and his life, he says, had been 'clouded by a thin drizzle of anxiety'.

I was sitting in a deck-chair out of doors at the back of Harper House. To my right was the lawn and a huge cedar tree. In front of me a few boys worked on their allotments, and beyond them lay the hard tennis court which was used chiefly for bicycle polo. The air smelt of sweet peas. A gramophone played in one of the studies behind me. And I began to be flooded with a ravishing sense of peace that flowed from the whole scene, rinsing away all impurities, gently rising and rising till I seemed to float, at one with the lawn and the sweet peas and the gramophone music and the blue sky on a deepening ecstasy where everything was to be loved, from which nothing was excluded but time. I do not know how long this experience lasted. The flood subsided as gently as it had risen, leaving no wrack behind it, no aftertaste of disillusion or melancholy. There had been a physical euphoria in it; but, overtopping this, lapping all round me, the sense of broader harmonies:

> The truth of flesh and spirit, sun and clay
> Singing for once together all in tune![3]

It was an experience of 'feeling good', of perfect harmony in which 'everything was to be loved': one of those serene and blessed moods which, in famous lines, Wordsworth thought

> . . . have no slight or trivial influence
> On that best portion of a good man's life,
> His little, nameless, unremembered, acts
> Of kindness and of love.

For Wordsworth, nature both was the great healer and the great teacher: solitary communing with earth and sky prepared the Wanderer

        . . . to receive
Deeply the lesson deep of love which he,
Whom Nature, by whatever means, has taught
To feel intensely, cannot but receive.

Here now is part of a longer and more detailed account of
the experience in which, coincidentally, sparrows again play
a part. It followed, like C. Day Lewis's, a period of depression
which its author understood as spiritual aridity and religious
doubt. It also came, like others we have quoted, during convalescence from physical illness: sickness and health in body,
mind and spirit are connected in ways yet little understood.
Margaret Montague had suffered a painful operation and is
here describing twenty minutes, more or less, when her hospital
bed was wheeled out on to the veranda for the first time after
the operation.

It was an ordinary cloudy March day. I am glad to think that it
was. I am glad to remember that there was nothing extraordinary
about the weather, nor any unusualness of setting – no flush of
spring or beauty of scenery – to induce what I saw. It was, on the
contrary, almost a dingy day. The branches were bare and colourless, and the occasional half-melted piles of snow were a forlorn
gray rather than white. Colourless little city sparrows flew and
chirped in the trees, while human beings, in no way remarkable,
passed along the porch.

There was, however, a wind blowing, and if any outside thing
intensified the experience, it was the blowing of that wind. In
every other respect it was an ordinary commonplace day. Yet here,
in this everyday setting, and entirely unexpectedly (for I had never
dreamed of such a thing), my eyes were opened, and for the first
time in all my life I caught a glimpse of the ecstatic beauty of
reality.

I cannot now recall whether the revelation came suddenly or
gradually; I only remember finding myself in the very midst of
those wonderful moments, beholding life for the first time in all its
young intoxication of loveliness, in its unspeakable joy, beauty and
importance. I cannot say exactly what the mysterious change was.
I saw no new thing, but I saw all the usual things in a miraculous
new light – in what I believe is their true light. I saw for the first
time how wildly beautiful and joyous, beyond any words of mine
to describe, is the whole of life. Every human being moving across
that porch, every sparrow that flew, every branch tossing in the
wind, was caught in and was a part of the whole mad ecstasy of
loveliness, of joy, of importance, of intoxication of life . . .

For those glorified moments I was in love with every living thing before me – the trees in the wind, the little birds flying, the nurses, the internes, and the people who came and went. There was nothing that was alive that was not a miracle. Just to be alive was itself a miracle. My very soul flowed out of me in a great joy.

The experience completed, one might say, the author's spiritual convalescence. It enabled her to regain her usual cheerful, kindly self and an untroubled faith in an all-powerful and benevolent deity and his purpose for the world. The experience had no specifically religious content, – no vision of saint or voice of command – though it was clearly of a kind to help make meaningful esoteric equations like 'God is Love'. Similarly it contained no specifically moral precepts though it may have made an unselfish altruism easier by relaxing a rather obsessional and guilt-ridden personality apt, as she says, to 'worry over sin'.

In what I saw there was nothing seemingly of an ethical nature. There were no new rules of conduct revealed by those twenty minutes. Indeed, it seemed as though beauty and joy were more at the heart of Reality than an over-anxious morality.[4]

The poet W. B. Yeats also knew experiences of unclouded euphoria when he felt affection for all the world and reflects on them in an essay published in 1918.

At certain moments, always unforeseen, I become happy, most commonly when at hazard I have opened some book of verse. Sometimes it is my own verse when, instead of discovering new technical flaws, I read with all the excitement of the first writing. Perhaps I am sitting in some crowded restaurant, the open book beside me, or closed, my excitement having overbrimmed the page. I look at the strangers near as if I had known them all my life, and it seems strange that I cannot speak to them: everything fills me with affection, for I have no longer any fears or any needs; I do not even remember that this happy mood must come to an end. It seems as if the vehicle had suddenly grown pure and far extended and so luminous that the images from 'Anima Mundi', embodied there and drunk with that sweetness, would, like a country drunkard who has thrown a wisp into his own thatch, burn up time.[5]

A kind of innocence and absence of hatred, he goes on to say, mark these blessed moods. He hesitates to ascribe them to love for love may be tainted with desire and

Desire itself is movement
Not in itself desirable.

Fifteen years after this essay Yeats published a poem in which he celebrated one such experience of love beyond desire which, like Margaret Montague's, lasted 'twenty minutes more or less'.

> My fiftieth year had come and gone,
> I sat, a solitary man,
> In a crowded London shop,
> An open book and empty cup
> On the marble table-top.
> While on the shop and street I gazed
> My body of a sudden blazed;
> And twenty minutes more or less
> It seemed so great my happiness,
> That I was blessed and could bless.[6]

The essay, though apparently written first – before his fiftieth birthday, in fact – is really an extended footnote to the late poem. With his own private, esoteric mythology, it is not surprising that Yeats' commentary is free of any religious concept or doctrine, but we turn now to three quotations in which the account of the experience is clearly coloured by the authors' Christian beliefs. All three, curiously, are connected with railway journeys and – surely commendable in an age of ecumenism – they represent a variety of denominations.

The first is from Hugh Fausset's *A Modern Prelude*. His mother died in giving him birth and he has described a boyhood overshadowed by the tyrannies, obsessions and reproaches of his grief-unhinged clergyman father in a home that was often a 'terrifying vortex of nerve storms'. It is a painful story, grimmer if anything than Butler's *Way of All Flesh* translated into reality. It was during the year between leaving Sedburgh School and going up to Cambridge that there began for the author a spiritual dawn in the form of experiences with nature of both a terrifying and a beatific kind which converted him to Wordsworth. And then, two years later, after the death of his father, he had an experience which he says first taught him the meaning of supernatural grace.

It came unsought to me, as I was sitting in one of the side chapels of Westminster Cathedral. Having three-quarters of an hour to spare before my train left Victoria, I had sought a refuge there from the noise of the streets. Fixing my eyes on a point of light in front of me, I had emptied my mind and the tension of feeling and thought was wholly relaxed. Before long I became conscious of a subtle change stealing over me. It was as if I was a cup which was slowly being filled with living water. I was invaded by some Will in which was infinite love and peace, wisdom and power. I felt a never previously known humility and gladness, an expressible certainty that behind and within all the discords of life there was a divine intention and a final harmony; that the darkness in me was in this timeless moment resolved in light and the error redeemed in ultimate comprehension. It was I that comprehended, yet it was not I. For a spirit possessed me, so that I did not know myself, but only the reality of which I was a centre and the Eternal Unity which had taken me to itself.

And the virtue of the experience remained with me long after I had left the Cathedral. It was as if a knot had been untied in my being, a veil withdrawn. The crowded streets and station were luminous, and I felt for my fellow passengers an ineffable love which passed through the mask of personality, the outer barrier of the petulant face or uncomely features, to the real being within.[7]

This experience filled him with 'a sense of wonderful well-being' in which he was 'desireless' yet possessed of all he could desire. The tide of inspiration lasted twenty-four hours before beginning to ebb, 'yet inwardly I was not the same nor ever could be again'. It led him ultimately beyond Christianity towards a life-long study of oriental religions.

The second example comes from Canon Raven's auto-biography A Wanderer's Way. He describes himself at school, where he was neither popular nor happy, as being, 'a prig, a prude, a bookworm and a bug-hunter'. At Cambridge he experienced a delayed spring of nature-mystical rapture and ecstasy. After university, unsure of his vocation, he went to Liverpool as Assistant Secretary for Secondary Education. He was, he says, 'thoroughly lay, full of secular interests', finding pious people irritating and the recital of offices a bore. He first made real contact with poverty in helping to run a City Youth Club and he calls it 'a crucial period of my life'. Then came a series of events leading up to the turning point of his life.

Finally there was a visit to my friend of college days, who had now taken orders and was a curate at Stoke on Trent. Liverpool has its squalid streets, and I was used to slums. But for brute ugliness Stoke and its vast and dismal churchyard stand unique. My friend was ill: I wandered up to his rooms alone, and the grim tragedy of the place struck me cold with misery. He had loved the country and music, and all beautiful things: and he was living in this hell. I found him, and behold he was not alone. No other phrase will express it. Here walking with him in the midst of the furnace was Jesus: and its flames were an aureole . . .

That day was decisive . . . Since I had seen him, he had found Jesus, and the effect of the discovery was manifest. His whole direction and outlook were altered under the new influence: there was joy and quiet confidence in his face, purpose in his life, sympathy and strength in all his actions. Jesus was alive and present to my friend as He had been to the eleven in the upper room. He was alive and present to me . . . Such is a summary of the crucial event of my life . . .

There have been two great episodes in my life spent in trains: the first was when I travelled back from my lady's home in Norfolk and knew that she loved me; the second was the journey that evening from Stoke to Liverpool. And the peculiar quality of them both was the same. It was a glory of wonder and worship, an overwhelming surprise that to me, to me of all people in the world, this comradeship of love had been given; an awe, free from all fear and all desire, utterly happy in the certainty of the gift; a rapture in which there was neither past nor future, a rapture full of the song of the morning stars.[8]

Once again, the love and rapture he felt was 'free from all desire'. Raven says of this event which was the turning point of his life:

I have naturally examined it as thoroughly and tested it as ruthlessly as I can. No one wants to build his life on an illusion, still less does he want to persuade others to accept an illusion as a fact.

He scrupulously considers all the sceptical or 'scientific' explanations – nerves, imagination, auto-suggestion, wish-fulfilment, hallucination – for his experience, in a longish chapter from which I have only picked out and strung together three short paragraphs.

Finally, in this group, here is a less disjointed quotation from Leslie Weatherhead, who is also defensively aware of the tendency of some psychologists to produce reductionist explanations for man's most life- and faith-enhancing experiences. He says that he would not call himself a mystic but has had half-a-dozen experiences, of which he describes just one, which made him certain that all of us are 'in the hands of a Mysterious Power which is utterly friendly', and that 'in the end good will triumph over every form of evil'.

Vauxhall Station on a murky November Saturday evening is not the setting one would choose for a revelation of God! I was a young theological student aged nineteen, being sent from Richmond Theological College (London University) to take the services somewhere – I cannot remember where – for some minister in a Greater London church who had fallen ill. The third-class compartment was full. I cannot remember any particular thought processes which may have led up to the great moment. It is possible that I was ruminating over the sermons I had prepared, and feeling – what I have always felt – how inadequate they were to 'get over' to others what I really felt about the Christian religion and its glorious message.

But the great moment came and when, years later, I read C. S. Lewis's *Surprised by Joy*. I thought, 'Yes, I know exactly how he felt. I felt like that'. For a few seconds only, I suppose, the whole compartment was filled with light. This is the only way I know in which to describe the moment, for there was nothing to *see* at all. I felt caught up into some tremendous sense of being within a loving, triumphant and shining purpose. I never felt more humble. I never felt more exalted. A most curious, but overwhelming sense possessed me and filled me with ecstasy. I felt that all was well for all mankind – how poor the words seem! The word 'well' is so poverty stricken. All men were shining and glorious beings who in the end would enter incredible joy. Beauty, music, joy, love immeasurable and a glory unspeakable, all this they would inherit. Of this they were heirs. My puny message, if I passed my exams and qualified as a minister, would contribute only an infinitesimal drop to the ocean of love and truth which God wanted men to enjoy, but my message was of the same *nature* as that ocean. I was right to want to be a minister. I had wanted to be a doctor and the conflict had been intense, but in that hour I knew the ministry was the right path for me. For me it was right, right, right . . . An indescribable joy possessed me . . .

All this happened over fifty years ago but even now I can see myself in the corner of that dingy, third-class compartment with the feeble lights of inverted gas mantles overhead and the Vauxhall platforms outside with milk cans standing there. In a few moments the glory had departed – all but one curious, lingering feeling. I *loved* everybody in that compartment.[9]

As with Canon Raven, Weatherhead's experience of love

beyond desire in the railway compartment settled once and for all his doubts about his vocation and again he goes on to compare it to great moments of contact with nature and art. Happy the man, we might exclaim, who finds such a source of faith and optimism: happy he who finds himself flooded with love for all mankind. And we might speak more truly than we realize for happiness may be the secret of the good life. Certainly Spinoza held that 'Happiness is not the reward of virtue, but virtue itself; and we do not enjoy happiness because we control our desires, but it is because we enjoy it that we are able to control them.'

At this point a word of caution is necessary: the feeling that we are overflowing with happiness, love and benevolence for all mankind may not, in fact, flow over into benevolent behaviour at all; it may be a delusion. Aldous Huxley and Colin Wilson have both described the overwhelming sense of love, trust, innocence and benevolence they felt after taking mescalin but, whereas Huxley is optimistic about the effect of such an experience on a man's subsequent actions, Wilson thinks it more likely to result in passivity, physical enfeeblement and a dangerous spiritual hubris. R. E. L. Masters and Jean Houston in their careful study, *The Varieties of Psychedelic Experience*[10] show that young members of the drug movement frequently make claims to personal apotheosis and enlightenment which would be funny if they were not so horrendous in their conceit. They somewhat facetiously coin the phrase 'galloping agape' to describe the deluded state of mind of the hippy who believes himself to be full of gentleness and love for all the universe when his overt behaviour is surly, selfish and irresponsible. He could be paralleled, of course, by the pious and self-righteous do-gooder who is officious, insensitive and interfering. We cannot too often remind ourselves of Paul's words, 'By their fruits shall ye know them.' Masters and Houston still maintain that sometimes, though they think not frequently, an authentic religious experience (according to criteria which they state) may occur within the context of the psychedelic drug state. As I have said in the introduction, it would certainly be a supreme irony in the history of religion if anyone at any time swallowing a pill could achieve what has been rarely attained by a lifetime of 'prayer, observance, discipline, thought and action'.

The experience of love beyond desire is not the prerogative of Christians, as this chapter has made clear. Its value in moral terms will depend on whether or not it results in increments of kindness, moral strength, sensitivity and so forth in an operative degree. This is a difficult empirical question about which there seems all too little hard evidence. The experience can certainly strengthen faith, as the testimony of Canon Raven and Leslie Weatherhead make clear, and when that faith is inextricably connected with ethical injunctions like loving one's neighbour it may be more helpful in leading a better life than holding other religious beliefs or none. But to say this is to say something about the moral value of Christian teaching rather than about the experience itself.

Finally, let us end this chapter with a quotation from Ida Gandy's account of her upbringing in a Wiltshire vicarage. It will remind us again of what has been so amply seen in earlier chapters, namely that children sense that 'love beyond desire' which belongs to the timeless world of spirit first in their mother's arms but then in their dealings with the visible, tangible, temporal world of meadow grove and stream rather than in the scripture lesson or church service. Good Friday mornings, she says, with their too familiar tale of Christ's suffering, the melancholy hymns and the prospect of boiled parsnips and salt cod for lunch, cast a shadow over the blue sky outside, the budding trees and the bird-song.

But all the same, events now took a new turn. For it was our custom on Good Friday afternoon to sally forth with baskets in search of flowers wherewith to decorate the church for Easter, and every year we went the same way; indeed, to choose any other would have seemed a wanton defiance of all Good Friday traditions.

The chastening influences of the morning were not cast away in a moment, and we would start northwards up the steep chalk hill rather soberly, hugging to ourselves the thought that after all this expedition was not just for our own satisfaction; that Christ would be pleased with us for wanting to make the church look beautiful.

But I am bound to say that this thought grew fainter and fainter as we proceeded on our journey.

Once we stood at the top of the hill with the unfettered downs spread north, east, and west about us we were conscious of being back in our own world again. Our spirits rose with a bound. That other world, where sad-looking people stood under a cross and let Christ's blood 'drop gently on them drop by drop', ceased to exist for us, or grew as remote as the vale below when an east wind shrouded it in mist. *This* was the real world – this world where larks sprang heavenwards on all sides, where purple shadows flew over the hills, where peewits ran through the grass with lifted crests, and the broken music of sheep-bells floated on the wind. Death – our own, anyone's – became incredible . . .

The first thrush's nest, the first bit of ground-ivy spreading its purple-blue blossoms under a sheltered hedge, the first coltsfoot gleaming in an upland field, these were things to make our hearts leap. And I can remember, in a little boggy wood one March evening, laying the first primrose against my cheek with such a passion of love filling me that all the beauty and fragrance of the world seemed gathered in that soft pale face.[11]

6 *The Distraction Fit*

In September 1765 Rousseau retreated from persecutions, real and imaginary, to the little island of Saint-Pierre in the lake of Bienne. There he enjoyed an idyllic but all too short respite, 'freed from the earthly passions engendered by the tumult of social life' and from what Vaughan calls 'the dirty devices of this world'. He determined, for the remainder of his days 'to live without restraints and eternally at leisure. Such is the life of the blessed in the other world, and henceforth I thought of it as my supreme felicity in this.' It was, in fact, less than two months before the Bernese authorities forced him to resume his wanderings which, in the following January, brought him to England where he wrote his *Confessions*. But for a few weeks on his island he enjoyed perfect tranquillity and devoted his time to botanizing, 'luxurious indolence' and 'delicious musings'.

As evening drew on, I used to come down from the high ground and sit on the beach at the water's brink in some hidden sheltering place. There the murmur of the waves and their agitation, charmed all my senses and drove every other movement away from my soul; they plunged it into delicious dreamings, in which I was often surprised by night. The flux and reflux of the water, its ceaseless stir swelling and falling at intervals, striking on ear and sight, made up for the internal movements which my musings extinguished; they were enough to give me delight in mere existence, without taking any trouble of thinking. From time to time arose some passing thought of the instability of the things of this world, of which the face of the waters offered an image; but such light impressions were swiftly effaced in the uniformity of the ceaseless motion, which rocked me as in a cradle; it held me with such fascination that even when called at the hour and by the signal appointed, I could not tear myself away without summoning all my force.[1]

Here on Saint-Pierre he experienced what he calls the 'single sense of existence' in which the 'present has no ending' and wherein is neither privation nor delight, desire nor apprehension. It was 'happiness full, perfect, and sufficing, that leaves in the Soul no conscious unfilled void'.

Rousseau was careful to distinguish his idleness-in-solitude from the idleness of society which he had escaped from and which he compares to the boring labour of a galley slave. Wordsworth, too, knew that what appeared idleness and unprofitable hours to the world in general and to schoolmasters in particular – as when, for instance, at dusk by Windermere he

> Blew mimic hootings to the silent owls
> That they might answer him –

could be 'more prodigal of blessings' than busyness as the world judges. Rousseau's description of how in his reverie his (too literally translated) 'internal movements' were extinguished by the sight and sound of lapping water inevitably prompts comparison with the lines from 'Tintern Abbey':

> ... the breath of this corporeal frame
> And even the motion of our human blood
> Almost suspended, we are laid asleep
> In body, and become a living soul.

57

In earlier chapters, particularly in 'The Impossible Union', we have seen examples of people who momentarily 'lost' themselves or for whom joy seemed to rise to the point of ecstasy in the strict sense of standing outside oneself. In this chapter we shall look at some further examples of more prolonged trances or trance-like states.

Rousseau says that he 'could not mark the point that cut off dream from reality' and it seems that reverie, dream, trance and perhaps even fainting and catalepsy may sometimes shade imperceptibly into one another. A flickering light may precipitate a migraine or even an epileptic fit just as the ripples on the lake fascinated Rousseau; their murmuring lulled him into oblivion like the voice of a hypnotist. We have seen in chapter 2 how Andrew Young could induce a visionary waking dream by repeating to himself 'I see what I am seeing'. Tennyson provides another example of auto-hypnosis in which individuality was dissolved away by the device of repeating his own name.

> I have never had any revelations through anaesthetics, but a kind of waking trance – this for lack of a better word – I have frequently had, quite up from boyhood, when I have been all alone. This has come upon me through repeating my own name to myself silently, till all at once, as it were out of the intensity of the consciousness of individuality, individuality itself seemed to dissolve and fade away into boundless being, and this not a confused state but the clearest, the surest of the surest, utterly beyond words – where death was an almost laughable impossibility – the loss of personality (if so it were) seeming no extinction, but the only true life. I am ashamed of my feeble description. Have I not said the state is utterly beyond words?
>   . . . By God Almighty! there is no delusion in the matter! It is no nubulous ecstasy, but a state of transcendent wonder, associated with absolute clearness of mind.[2]

Tennyson's self-induced experience was one of transcendent wonder in which death was a laughable impossibility, but not all trance-like states are wholly agreeable nor can they be brought on voluntarily.

During our excursions on the downs, nature began to influence my imagination in a peculiar way. When the light of evening was falling, or when we found ourselves in some secluded corner, with a prospect towards the Bristol Channel and the Welsh hills, I passed from the sense of a tangible present into dream. This was a very definite phase of experience, approaching hypnotism in its character. I partly dreaded the subjugation of my conscious will, and partly looked forward to it with a thrill of exquisite anticipation. I learned to recognise the symptoms of this on-coming mood. But I could not induce it by an act of volition. It needed some specific touch of the external world upon my sensibility.[3]

J. A. Symonds was writing here of his childhood: later – as we shall see in chapter 12 – his trances became marked by the wholly terrifying sense first of the obliteration of external reality and finally of dissolution of the conscious self. With these examples of contemporaries like Tennyson and Symonds in mind, it is not surprising that at different times and places in history trances have been variously interpreted as the intrusion of baneful spirits to be treated by exorcism or as joyful Dionysian epiphanies to be invoked by all manner of strenuous rituals.

Frank Conroy's experience seems to combine elements of frightening dissolution of the conscious will with paradisiacal ecstasy. He seems also to have discovered accidentally a technique of contemplation when, at about the age of twelve, he used to hide from the rest of his family by curling up inside the miniature world of a dog-kennel.

I drifted through the hours wrapped in a cloud of absent-mindedness. Faintly dizzy, half asleep, and beyond time, I slipped gradually out of the world.

A buzzing inside my head. My body is far away, much too far to respond to my wishes. I stare at my fingers curled on the floor. Immense, swollen fingers, weighty as sandbags. They are dead. I see nothing except exactly what I am looking at, as if I were watching the world through a tube. When I shift my glance to the floor a few inches below my hand, my thumb and index finger disappear.

It occurs to me that if I want to come back I'd better do it now because in a few moments it'll be too late. Instantly I relax, letting myself be swept away. I don't want to come back. The buzzing increases, swallowing me, drowning me until a mysterious change of frequency occurs and I come through into the clear, up above the buzzing into a silent, calm world, my heart bursting with happiness.

Paradise! Light! Air! I am extended over vast spaces like a pure white cloud, drifting freely, rolling exuberantly in the sunlight high above the earth. I sail through the blue! I am everywhere![4]

The next two examples belong to adolescence rather than childhood and are associated more or less directly with religion. Both experiences seem to have been self-induced, though not wholly consciously so, and both only reach the brink of trance before receding. The first is from Edmund Gosse's *Father and Son*. He had been brought up in the Plymouth Brotherhood to be devoutly pious and is here writing of himself at the age of sixteen when he was also haunted by visions of sensuous beauty and pouring out pietistic verses on biblical and evangelical subjects. He was alone on a summer evening watching the approaching sunset from an upper window of his boarding school, all the other pupils having gone for a walk in charge of an usher.

There was an absolute silence below and around me; a magic of suspense seemed to keep every topmost twig from waving.

Over my soul there swept an immense wave of emotion. Now, surely, now the great final change must be approaching. I gazed up into the tenderly coloured sky, and I broke irresistibly into speech. 'Come now, Lord Jesus', I cried, 'Come now and take me to be for ever with Thee in Thy Paradise. I am ready to come. My heart is purged from sin, there is nothing that keeps me rooted to this wicked world. Oh, come now, now and take me before I have known the temptations of life, before I have to go to London and all the dreadful things that happen there!' And I raised myself on the sofa, and leaned upon the window-sill, and waited for the glorious apparition.

This was the highest moment of my religious life, the apex of my striving after holiness. I waited a while, watching; and then I felt a faint shame at the theatrical attitude I had adopted, although I was alone. Still I gazed and still I hoped. Then a little breeze sprang up and the branches danced. Sounds began to rise from the road beneath me. Presently the colour deepened, the evening came on. From far below there rose to me the chatter of the boys returning home. The tea-bell rang, – last word of prose to shatter my mystical poetry. 'The Lord has not come, the Lord will never come', I muttered, and in my heart the artificial edifice of extravagant faith began to totter and crumble.[5]

The language Gosse uses to describe this 'highest moment' of his religous life, particularly when he says 'My unwholesome excitement, bubbling up in this violent way, reached at last a climax and foamed over', suggests that he was not wholly unaware of the erotic analogue of his experience.

The second example is from Forrest Reid, who was a year or two older. His mind was full of the pagan deities of the Greeks rather than evangelical Christianity and, possibly, physiologically, his experience may have been closer to swooning though there is the same straining after the divine afflatus, the same yearning for union or to be ravished into a metaphorical if not literal heaven.

It was June, and I was supposed to be working for an intermediate examination, and had a book or two with me even on this blazing afternoon. It was hot and still. The breathless silence seemed unnatural, seemed, as I lay motionless in the tangled grass, like a bridge that reached straight back into the heart of some dim antiquity. I had a feeling of uneasiness, of unrest though I lay so still – of longing and excitement and expectation: I had a feeling that some veil might be drawn away, that there might come to me something, some one . . .

My body seemed preternaturally sensitive, my blood moved quickly, I had an extraordinary feeling of struggle, as if some power were struggling to reach me as I was trying to reach it, as if there *was* something there, something waiting, if only I could get through. At that moment I longed for a sign, some definite and direct response, with a longing that was a kind of prayer. And a strange thing happened. For though there was no wind, a little green leafy branch was snapped off from the tree above me, and fell to the ground at my hand. I drew my breath quickly; there was a drumming in my ears; I knew that the green woodland before me was going to split asunder, to swing back on either side like two great painted doors . . . And then – then I hesitated, blundered, drew back, failed. The moment passed, was gone, and at first gradually, and then rapidly, I felt the world I had so nearly reached slipping from me, till at last there was all around me only a pleasant summer scene, through which, from the hidden river below, there rose the distant voices and laughter of a passing boating-party.[6]

Forrest Reid does not comment directly on this experience or attempt to explain it but in a subsequent volume of reminiscences written more than twenty years later he says:

I have never believed in any formal religion, but I have experienced an emotion that seemed to me religious. In a chapter in 'Apostate' I tried to describe this, but I have been told that I merely described a landscape and a mood, and that the mood had nothing whatever to do with religion. Be this as it may, it was my nearest approach to it, and it was created by some power outside myself.[7]

Forrest Reid is only one of many who have had this strong sense of powers or presences all around us, of another order of reality waiting to be discovered if only we knew how to break through to it. Wordsworth had experienced

> . . . Such visitings
> Of awful promise, when the light of sense
> Goes out in flashes that have shewn to us
> The invisible world.

He had felt the presence of 'unknown modes of being' too strongly ever wholly to discount their real existence. He is often pictured in biographies as having become timid, cautious and orthodox in middle age, but when he was nearly seventy, in lines prefaced to 'The White Doe of Rylstone', he wrote,

> Oh! there is a life that breathes not; powers there are
> That touch each other to the quick in modes
> Which the gross world no sense hath to perceive,
> No soul to dream of.

Generally it is 'some*thing* far more deeply interfused' in nature that he senses rather than some divine presence and it is only occasionally and, one cannot help feeling, as an afterthought, that he associates these powers and presences with the Christian God.

If Gosse and Forrest Reid hesitated, stumbled and retreated from the brink of trance, A. E. (George Russell) seems to have been a totally immersed and life-long nature mystic. The style of *The Candle of Vision* is curiously high-flown for one who, apart from being an artist and poet, was for many years employed in something as earthy as the organization of the Agricultural Co-operative Movement in Ireland. A. E. tells his tale 'with fringes and tassels', as the Italians say. But if the dithyrambics he adopts make the reader doubt the authenticity of his experiences, then there is ample testimony from his friends and contemporaries – particularly in George Moore's autobiography *Hail and Farewell* – that he was frequently lost to the world, literally entranced in converse with the Immortals, Druids and other shadowy figures which haunted his imagination. These trances might come unsought or, more frequently, he might induce them to establish that sense of what Willa Muir calls 'belonging to the universe'. On one occasion he returned after a year in the city to his cottage at Steep in Hampshire. It was late and he was tired with travelling but still restless.

> So I stole out of the cottage and over the dark ridges to the place of rocks, and sat down, and let the coolness of the night chill and still the fiery dust in the brain. I waited trembling for the faintest touch, the shyest breathing of the Everlasting within my soul, the sign of reception and forgiveness. I knew it would come. I could not so desire what was not my own, and what is our own we cannot lose. Desire is hidden identity. The darkness drew me heavenward. From the hill the plains beneath slipped away grown vast and vague, remote and still. I seemed alone with immensity, and there came at last that melting of the divine darkness into the life within me for which I prayed. Yes, I still belonged, however humbly, to the heavenly household. I was not outcast. Still, though by a thread fine as that by which a spider hangs from the rafters, my being was suspended from the habitations of eternity.[8]

Of one other trance, A. E. writes:

> Once, drawn by some inner impulse to meditate at an unusual hour, I found quick oblivion of the body. The blood and heat of the brain ebbed from me as an island fades in the mist behind a swift vessel fleeting into light. The ways were open within. I rose through myself and suddenly felt as if I had awakened from a dream.

Of the end of this trance he says, 'Something below drew me down and I was again an exile from the light.' Trances like his have a part in many of the world's religions and are often valued as providing direct experiential evidence of the divine or spirit world. They tend to be explained either as the temporary absence of the soul from the body while it is elevated into communion with the spirit world or as the possession of the body by spirits from that supernatural realm. These two interpretations of trance are not, of course, incompatible and can be held together. In Christianity, despite the ecstasies of St Teresa and other acknowledged mystics, trance has generally been regarded with suspicion and much more often interpreted as the work of the devil than any kind of divine revelation. When A. E. writes 'I rose through myself . . .', he suggests what might be called the 'ecstatic' rather than the 'possession' belief about his trance. The same is true of the final example – rather a macabre one – which we will look at in this chapter. It comes from Thomas De Quincey's *Autobiography*. At the age of six he has just done what was forbidden him and crept into the bedroom in which his nine-year-old sister is lying dead.

I stood checked for a moment; awe, not fear, fell upon me; and, whilst I stood, a solemn wind began to blow – the saddest that ear ever heard. It was a wind that might have swept the fields of mortality for a thousand centuries. Many times since, upon summer days, when the sun is about the hottest, I have remarked the same wind arising and uttering the same hollow, solemn, Memnonian, but saintly swell: it is in this world the one great audible symbol of eternity. And three times in my life have I happened to hear the same sound in the same circumstances – viz., when standing between an open window and a dead body on a summer day.

Instantly, when my ears caught this vast Aeolian intonation, when my eyes filled with the golden fulness of life, the pomps of the heavens above, or the glory of the flowers below, and turning when it settled upon the frost which overspread my sister's face, instantly a trance fell upon me. A vault seemed to open in the zenith of the far blue sky, a shaft which ran up for ever. I, in spirit, rose as if on billows that also ran up the shaft for ever; and the billows seemed to pursue the throne of God; but *that* also ran before us and fled away continually. The flight and the pursuit seemed to go on for ever and ever. Frost gathering frost, some Sarsar wind of death, seemed to repel me; some mighty relation between God and death dimly struggled to evolve itself from the dreadful antagonism between them; the shadowy meanings even yet continue to exercise and torment, in dreams, the deciphering oracle within me. I slept – for how long I cannot say; slowly I recovered my self-possession; and when I woke, I found myself standing, as before, close to my sister's bed.

I have reason to believe that a *very* long interval had elapsed during this wandering or suspension of my perfect mind.[9]

In a sceptical, scientific age experiences like this will be dismissed as fanciful or relegated to the province of abnormal psychology and regarded as 'unhealthy'. They may not ultimately prove unfathomable though until some convincing rational explanation is available of how and why the central nervous system should play such tricks on us, they will continue to be a mystery and to attract countless diverse interpretations.

7 Sudden Illumination

In the moments of trance and ecstasy quoted in earlier chapters there was often present the feeling of impending revelation, of doors about to be opened, mists dispersed, veils withdrawn and secrets disclosed. One remembers Edmund Gosse and Forrest Reid waiting in an agony of expectation for their respective deities to appear, or A. E. 'tormented by limitations of understanding' and convinced voices were speaking to him just out of earshot, or Margiad Evans as a small child muttering to herself, 'there is *something* out of doors'. 'When I walk in the fields,' said Charles Kingsley, 'I am oppressed now and then with an innate feeling that everything I see has a meaning, if I could but understand it. And this feeling of being surrounded with truths which I cannot grasp amounts to an indescribable awe sometimes.' As William James pointed out when commenting on this, such feelings are surely far from uncommon.

Equally commonly, the unattended moment is felt to have contained more than a hint of actual illumination, of being, as Morag Coate says, 'in touch with a reality beyond my own' or of 'mysteries made clear', as Richard Hillyer puts it. Of that night in Palestine, when Jacquetta Hawkes watched the caravan of camels swaying down the Wadi with the Mediterranean like a bar of silver in the distance, she said, 'the moonlight had ceased to be a physical thing and now represented a state of illumination in my own mind . . . it seemed that my thoughts and feelings had been given an extraordinary clarity and truth'.

This 'noetic' quality of having knowledge or insight into depths of truth unplumbed by the discursive intellect is, in William James' view, one of the four necessary characteristics of an experience (together with ineffability, transcience and passivity) which justify us in calling it 'mystical'. Let us look at some examples before getting too involved in the difficulties which arise from claiming access to knowledge which is ineffable.

As a very small child, Richard Church hoarded leaves, twigs, pebbles and feathers, which appealed to him, in 'blind faith that these moments of recognition, of mental groping, must mean something that one day I should be able to piece together, and make myself master of'. At the age of eleven, he had an experience which seems to have been every bit as cataclysmic as any of the distraction fits quoted in the last chapter, but it was also a revelation which was important for his faith and philosophy of life.

> My sense of Christ, whose nature had already dawned upon my infant consciousness some two years earlier, now became much more defined: I saw him as mind itself, the Me within myself . . . His body was the Word itself. My groping after this realisation was suddenly, miraculously rewarded one morning in school, during the first lesson of the day, which was always that odd subject called 'Scripture' . . .
>
> We had been set to learn a passage from one of Paul's Epistles by heart. I had already got this, and I sat turning the dreary-looking pages of the school edition of the Bible, covered in shiny black. One hand was thrust into my inside pocket, clasping the tiny silver watch as a talisman. The other stopped at the page opening on the Fourth Gospel. I saw the phrase, 'In the beginning was the Word, and the Word was with God, and the Word was God.'
>
> I felt the hair on my head tingling, and a curtain of red blood appeared to fall before my eyes. I leaned forward clasping myself close, while the world rocked around me. And as this earthquake subsided, I saw a new skyline defined. It was a landscape in which objects and words were fused. All was one, with the word as the verbal reality brought to material life by Mind, by man. It was therefore the very obvious, tangible presence of the Creator.
>
> Sitting in Surrey Lane School, crouched over my fluttering and burning stomach, with one hand still clasping the silver watch given me by my mother, I received a philosophy which I have never lost, a working faith in the oneness of all life.[1]

Richard Church's physical sensations seem like a combination of fainting, vertigo and the aesthetic *frisson* but, rather exceptionally, he does not find it too difficult to say what the truth was that was revealed to him. Perhaps this makes his experience less like the revelations of St John and St Teresa and more like one of those 'acts of creation' catalogued by

Arthur Koestler, or simply an example, in acute form, of that breakthrough to comprehension of an abstract notion for which teachers must often impotently pray on behalf of their pupils. Nevertheless, the experience had a life-shaping importance for him: 'Everything was now contained, for me, in the power of the Word . . . The knowledge was a fire within me, lighting my mind, consuming my body.' And it gave him 'authority over the horrors, the divisions, the guilt complexes, that beset us all as we go through life, in a world supposedly split into two, the flesh and the spirit, where civil war rages eternally, in sombre Miltonic gloom and hopelessness'. To this extent it was not only life-shaping but redemptive and regenerative in a way that is certainly analogous to religious conversion.

Arthur Koestler was a little older than Richard Church when he had an experience which he calls a mystic elation and which was similarly noetic and life shaping.

One day during the summer holidays, in 1919, I was lying on my back under a blue sky on a hill slope in Buda. My eyes were filled with the unbroken, unending, transparent, complacent, saturated blue above me, and I felt a mystic elation – one of those states of spontaneous illumination which are so frequent in childhood and become rarer and rarer as the years wear on. In the middle of this beatitude, the paradox of spatial infinity suddenly pierced my brain as if it had been stung by a wasp. You could shoot a super-arrow into the blue with a super-force which could carry it beyond the pull of earth's gravity, past the moon, past the sun's attraction – and what then? It would traverse inter-stellar space, pass other suns, other galaxies, Milky Ways, Honeyed Ways, Acid Ways – and what then? It would go on and on and on past the spiral nebulae, and more galaxies and more spiral nebulae, and there would be nothing to stop it, no limit and no end, in space or in time – and the worst of it was that all this was not fantasy but literally true. Such an arrow could be made real . . . it was sheer torture to the brain. The sky had no business to look so blue and smug if its smile hid the most aweful secret which it was unwilling to yield, just as adults drove one crazy with their smile when they were determined to withhold a secret, cruelly and lawlessly denying one's most sacred right – the right to know.[2]

Not only the experience but the book also, it is interesting to notice, came before man had in fact launched an arrow into the blue – a rocket powerful enough to escape earth's gravity.

Imagination is not only what Wordsworth called it, 'the mightiest lever known to the moral world', but to the scientific world as well. The mind that imagined the myth of Icarus had made a first step on the road that led to space travel.

The importance Arthur Koestler attaches to this moment of sudden illumination in his childhood in Hungary is indicated by the fact that he takes the title of his book from it. The intellectual leap he had made is exactly like Richard Church's, though the truth that suddenly stung him like a wasp was a truth of physics rather than of metaphysics. From this moment he dates his conscious dedication of himself to science and his gnawing ambition to be the one to solve the unbearable riddle. It was the 'Romance' stage of his scientific education but – typical, I believe, of unattended moments – it had a unitive or integrative quality about it which refused to be narrowly channelled. A few pages later he writes: 'I had an absolute, unshakable conviction that there was a basic central mystery, related to eternity and the infinite, and that some fraction of the secret was contained in all great works of literature – that in fact their greatness and fame was due to their containing part of the mystery.' Koestler's experience was an imaginative excitement but the imagination is multi-faceted, like a well-cut diamond flashing in response to light from any quarter.

Jacquetta Hawkes was an adult, Richard Church a boy of eleven and Arthur Koestler fourteen when the sudden illumination came to them, but such experiences, seemingly, can occur at any age. Mary Antin was a tiny child (she does not say and probably did not remember precisely how old) in her native Poland.

In the long black furrows yet unsown a peasant pushed his plough. I watched him go up and down, leaving a new black line on the bank for every turn. Suddenly he began to sing, a rude plowman's song. Only the melody reached me, but the meaning sprang up in my heart to fit it – a song of the earth and the hopes of the earth. I sat a long time listening, looking, tense with attention. I felt myself discovering things. Something in me gasped for life, and lay still. I was but a little body, and Life Universal had suddenly burst upon me. For a moment I had my little hand on the Great Pulse, but my fingers slipped, empty. For the space of a wild heartbeat I *knew*, and then I was again a simple child, looking to

68

my earthly senses for life. But the sky had stretched for me, the earth had expanded; a greater life had dawned in me. We are not born all at once, but by bits. The body first, and the spirit later . . .[3]

For the space of a heart beat she *knew*, but what did she know, what did she see? 'Life Universal' is rather less easy to grasp and formulate than Koestler's glimpse of infinity; more like those moments in which Wordsworth says 'we see into the life of things', perhaps. Nor was it just because she was so young that she has difficulty in saying what she learnt. Another autobiographer, Mary Austin in *Earth Horizon*, which is written in the third person, describes experiences of the pressure of knowledge aching intolerably to escape through her. 'It is impossible to describe this experience,' she says, 'so nearly universal that we ought not to be without a proper terminology for it,' but she does describe how it began for her at the age of ten. It was her duty to look after her baby brother as soon as he woke in the mornings so that he would not disturb her dying father.

Mary would warm a bowl of bread and milk for them both, or, if the hired man were about, get it warm from the cow, and steal away to the first row of orchard trees, or down between the grape-vine trellises, which gave her always a still, ordered feeling, very comforting – the sort of feeling one gets from cloisters – and there George, once he was fed, would play about happily for a while, or, as the warm morning beams fell upon him, drop suddenly into little cat naps, and there the experience would happen. Mary would be watching the dew slip down the clover stems, or the white webby moons of spider webs made thick with diamond drops, and around her would steal a sense of innumerable bright events, of tingling and unattempted possibilities; there would be a sense of swelling, of billows coming and going, lifting and dying away – and then someone would come looking for her from the house to say that the grown-up breakfast was ready . . .
As she grew older, Mary began to know the billowing sense as the pressure of knowledge, all the knowledge in the world, pulsing just out of reach. It came up *inside* her, she was uplifted with it, rocked upon it – there were times when she could discern within it, dimly, the shapes of specific knowledge – all the knowledge in the world, hers, aching intolerably to escape through her . . . By the time she enrolled at the normal school, Mary had had a little experience of cooperating with her experience. She knew that this inward swelling could be contented less achingly if you treated it as an

entity, neither feared nor attempted to escape from it, but went along with it. It was, to some extent, self-directive; it had appetites for pictures or music or great poetry, which could be satisfied by being fed.[4]

It is interesting to compare this passage with the extract from Margaret Isherwood's *Search For Meaning* with which we ended chapter 3, in that both writers' experiences involved having care of a baby and may have included unrecognized maternal feelings. However, Mary Austin says here that it was a 'billowing' sensation – and, incidentally, she is not the only writer to use the word. In it she thought she dimly discerned the shapes of specific knowledge which evidently remained 'pulsing just out of reach'. In this sense her experience seems to have been typical: the mystic claims with the utmost unshakable conviction that ineffable knowledge, truth, reality has been revealed to him. Jacob Boehme said that 'In one quarter of an hour I saw and knew more than if I had been many years together at an University,' but if one asks *what* he learnt in that quarter of an hour, one gets a misty answer: 'the being of all things, the Byss and the Abyss . . . the eternal generation of the Holy Trinity . . . and how the fruitful bearing womb of eternity brought forth', and so on. Similarly Ignatius Loyola had a 'strange illumination', as he sat on the river bank outside the town of Manresa, in which more was revealed to him in one moment, so he says in his autobiography, than in all the rest of his sixty-two years. But if we ask what he learnt, it was 'certain things pertaining to the mysteries of the faith'; more than that, it seems, could not be said.

When Boehme's name cropped up in conversation Boswell recalls Johnson gruffly remarking that if the divine Jacob had seen unutterable things it was a pity he ever attempted to utter them. Johnson was the least mystical of men, with a robust commonsense, and it is easy to share his impatience with claims to knowledge which is incommunicable. Evidently the knowledge gained is non-propositional and the meaning unconceptualized: the temptation is to retort, in schoolmasterly fashion, that if one cannot say what one means one does not know what one means and dismiss all claims to noetic experiences or 'gnosis' as delusional. What is interesting is that the mystic is apparently unabashed by his inability to say what knowledge he has gained, so deep is his conviction that his experience has assured him of the existence of a realm of truths transcending the laws of everyday language and logic, a realm above 'the loquacious level which rationalism inhabits', as William James puts it. If everyone was colour-blind and only saw in shades of grey, as scientists assure us many animals do, but a few rare individuals for a few brief moments glimpsed the world in full colour, would they not be forced to say their vision was ineffable? The world to which they wished to communicate their experience would have no conception of colour and therefore no language for it.

Here is another example, from R. M. Bucke, whose colour-ful life included fighting Indians, crewing a Mississippi steam-boat, gold mining and being maimed by frostbite before he became Professor of Mental and Nervous Diseases and Superintendent of an asylum for the insane in Ontario. Like Mary Austin, he writes of his first-hand experiences in the third person.

It was in the early spring, at the beginning of his thirty-sixth year. He and two friends had spent the evening reading Wordsworth, Shelley, Keats, Browning, and especially Whitman. They parted at midnight, and he had a long drive in a hansom (it was in an English city). His mind, deeply under the influence of the ideas, images and emotions called up by the reading and talk of the evening, was calm and peaceful. He was in a state of quiet, almost passive enjoyment. All at once, without warning of any kind, he found himself wrapped around as it were by a flame-coloured cloud. For an instant he thought of fire, some sudden conflagration in the great city; the next, he knew that the light was within himself. Directly afterwards came upon him a sense of exultation, of immense joyousness accompanied or immediately followed by an intellectual illumina-tion quite impossible to describe. Into his brain streamed one momentary lightning-flash of the Brahmic Splendour which has ever since lightened his life; upon his heart fell one drop of Brahmic Bliss, leaving thence-forward for always an after-taste of heaven. Among other things he did not come to believe, he *saw* and *knew* that the Cosmos is not dead matter but a living Presence, that the soul of man is immortal, that the universe is so built and ordered that without any peradventure all things work together for the good of each and all, that the foundation principle of the world is what we call love and that the happiness of every one is in the long run absolutely certain. He claims that he learned more within the few seconds during which the illumination lasted than in previous months or even years of study, and that he learned much that that no study could ever have taught.[5]

Bucke was thirty-six years old and he has a theory that such experiences of 'cosmic consciousness', as he calls it, usually occur in the prime of life, around the mid point of our three score years and ten. His experience, which was momentary and never repeated, was one of rapture, bliss and assurance of immortality. The revelation that 'the Cosmos is not dead matter' links it with Mary Austin's experience of 'Life Universal' quoted earlier in this chapter and with all those experiences of 'impossible union' in chapter 4, as well as being another 'intellectual illumination quite impossible to describe'.

Sometimes, when a writer says an experience was ineffable what he means, we may suspect, is that his experience contained apparently conflicting elements. He wants to say, perhaps, that it was at one and the same time joyful and sad or that he felt simultaneously humble and exalted and, feeling the coercive force of logical rules, he calls his experience 'ineffable' rather than be forced into logical contradictions. We are all, of course, perfectly familiar with paradoxes which are no problem to the religious mind, dying into life, the richness of poverty, loving one's enemy and so on, and the experience of art can be logically odd in a similar way. Aristotle puzzled over the exhilarating effect of witnessing tragic events portrayed in the theatre and his quasi-medical explanation of emotional purgation is only partly convincing. The experience of a great painting or musical work is also ineffable; what it means to us is not to be expressed in any form other than that employed by the artist himself.

What the man, like R. M. Bucke, who confidently claims a revelation of incommunicable knowledge is doing, it seems, is not merely blaming the inadequacy of language and declaring the irrelevance of normal prose statement, but dethroning reason from its solitary eminence. He is, with Pascal, asserting an emphatic dualism: 'The last proceeding of reason is to recognize that there is an infinity of things which are beyond it.' To William Soutar, the Scottish poet, the reason is 'A fool, with tapers, coming in the night' compared to the 'unearthly glow' of mystic illumination by which alone Reality is seen.

> Nothing on earth in this unearthly glow
> Is chang'd; but we are chang'd by the intense
> Revealment, and our dull intelligence
> Stares upon truth, but cannot prove it so.[6]

For a last example in this chapter we will return to Arthur Koestler in a later volume of autobiography than *Arrow in the Blue*. He is an impressive witness, partly because he is a tough-minded scientist by training whose habitually empirical mind is forced by first-hand experience to take seriously as meaningful the 'nebulous gushings' of the mystics. In *The Invisible Writing* he describes his solitary confinement in a Spanish prison during the Civil War when he was expecting daily to be ordered out of his cell and executed for espionage. Here, in slightly abbreviated form, is his account of what happened.

I was standing at the recessed window of cell No. 40 and, with a piece of iron-spring that I had extracted from the wire mattress, was scratching mathematical formulae on the wall. Mathematics, in particular analytical geometry, had been the favourite hobby of my youth, neglected later on for many years. I was trying to remember how to derive the formula of the hyperbola, and was stumped; then I tried the ellipse and the parabola, and to my delight succeeded. Next I went on to recall Euclid's proof that the number of primes is infinite . . . Since I had become acquainted with Euclid's proof at school, it had always filled me with a deep satisfaction that was aesthetic rather than intellectual. Now, as I recalled the method and scratched the symbols on the wall, I felt the same enchantment.

And then, for the first time, I suddenly understood the reason for this enchantment: the scribbled symbols on the wall represented one of the rare cases where a meaningful and comprehensive statement about the infinite is arrived at by precise and finite means. The infinite is a mystical mass shrouded in a haze; and yet it was possible to gain some knowledge of it without losing oneself in treacly ambiguities. The significance of this swept over me like a wave. The wave had originated in an articulate verbal insight; but this evaporated at once, leaving in its wake only a wordless essence, a fragrance of eternity, a quiver of the arrow in the blue. I must have stood there for some minutes, entranced, with a wordless awareness that 'this is perfect – perfect'; until I noticed some slight mental discomfort nagging at the back of my mind –

some trivial circumstance that marred the perfection of the moment. Then I remembered the nature of that irrelevant annoyance: I was, of course, in prison and might be shot. But this was immediately answered by a feeling whose verbal translation would be: 'So what? Is that all? Have you got nothing more serious to worry about?', an answer so spontaneous, fresh and amused as if the intruding annoyance had been the loss of a collar-stud. Then I was floating on my back in a river of peace, under bridges of silence. It came from nowhere and flowed nowhere. Then there was no river and no I. The I had ceased to exist . . .

What distinguishes this type of experience from the emotional entrancements of music, landscape or love is that the former has a definitely intellectual, or rather noumenal, content. It is meaningful, though not in verbal terms. Verbal transcriptions that come nearest to it are: the unity and interlocking of everything that exists, an interdependence like that of gravitational fields or communicating vessels. The I ceases to exist because it has, by a kind of mental osmosis, established communication with, and been dissolved in, the universal pool. It is this process of dissolution and limitless expansion which is sensed as the 'oceanic feeling', as the draining of all tension, the absolute catharsis, the peace that passeth all understanding.

The coming back to the lower order of reality I found to be gradual, like waking up from anaesthesia. There was the question of the parabola scratched on the dirty wall, the iron bed and the iron table and the strip of blue Andalusian sky. But there was no unpleasant hangover as from other modes of intoxication. On the contrary: there remained a sustained and invigorating, serene and fear-dispelling after-effect that lasted for hours and days. It was as if a massive dose of vitamins had been injected into the veins. Or, to change the metaphor, I resumed my travels through my cell like an old car with its batteries freshly recharged.[7]

Koestler relates later on how these experiences filled him with feelings of altruism and of the essential dignity and equality of all men which is interesting in the light of our discussion of 'love beyond desire' in an earlier chapter. Interesting, too, are the analogies he draws between his experience in the prison and our experiences of nature and art as 'meaningful'.

T. S. Eliot said of sudden illumination – 'We had the experience but missed the meaning' and that as we approach the meaning we revive the experience in a different form, not as an isolated moment of happiness but as part of a pattern of timeless moments. Wordsworth would have said, I think, that to talk of missing the meaning at first is to miss the point, though he knew better than anybody the value of recollection in tranquillity. He had many moments of sudden illumination when

> ... all
> That I beheld respired with inward meaning

and his analysis of them is careful and detailed. They were invariably accompanied by an elevated mood, a 'shadowy exaltation' rather than mere happiness. They were important, in his view, not because of any *knowledge* he acquired but rather because

> ... the soul
> Remembering how she felt, but what she felt
> Remembering not, retains an obscure sense
> Of possible sublimity, to which,
> With growing faculties she doth aspire
> With faculties still growing, feeling still
> That whatsoever point they gain, they still
> Have something to pursue.

In that sense they were the foundation of hope, striving, altruism and ideals. To hope and strive is to be aware of that divine discontent on which the next chapter will focus.

8   The Spirit Unappeased

'There is hardly in the midst of our liveliest delights a single instant when the heart could tell us with real truth – "I would this instant might last for ever".' So says Rousseau in the fifth of his *Reveries* written at the end of his life. Joy, as we have noted before, is seldom if ever more than momentarily unalloyed: nowhere upon earth does the rose of happiness blossom without thorns. Rousseau goes on to ask: '. . . how can we give the name of happiness to a feeling state that all the

75

time leaves the heart unquiet and void, that makes us regret something gone, or still long for something to come?' It is on to this element of unquiet, regret and longing that we focus in this chapter.

As a boy, Wordsworth's search for joy was often restless and insatiable:

> In youth from rock to rock I went
> From hill to hill in discontent
> Of pleasures high and turbulent.

Later, as a young man, in his bitter disappointment with the course the French Revolution had taken, he was often

> more like a man
> Flying from something that he dreads than one
> Who sought the thing he loved.

Even his most intense moments were a '*shadowy* exaltation' because that 'obscure sense of possible sublimity' which they left behind was, I think it is fair to suppose, a kind of yearning. In a famous poem the seventeenth-century poet George Herbert saw this longing or 'repining restlesnesse' as a discontent which was indeed divine because it was a kind of 'pulley' by which God drew up human souls to himself where they might find rest. And Wordsworth, too, philosophically came to think of it as a source of aspiration, endeavour and spiritual growth, just as he comforted himself for the loss of his unattended moments with the thought that the memory of them remained a bliss of solitude. There were moments, however, when the sense of loss was almost as acute as the original moments and he was constrained to cry out

> Whither is fled the visionary gleam?
> Where is it now, the glory and the dream?

Very many other writers have found in the dregs of the cup of joy a bitter after-taste or, at best, a thirst unsatisfied. For A. L. Rowse (quoted in chapter 2) it was 'an unease of heart, some reaching out towards perfection such as impels men into religion, some sense of the transcendence of things . . .' And Richard Jefferies (quoted in chapter 1) said of his experience: 'When it ceased I did wish for some increase or enlargement of my existence to correspond with the largeness of feeling I had momentarily enjoyed.' An enlargement of existence – that has been the longing of romantics in all ages, and one never satisfied for

> . . . 'tis a thing impossible to frame
> Conceptions equal to the Soul's desires.

'Thou would'st not seek me if thou had'st not already found me' is a famous paradox of Pascal. Possibly Blake had it in mind when he wrote: 'Man's Desires are limited by his Perceptions; none can desire what he has not perceived.' There is no knowing what such visionaries had perceived. Did not Blake say he had seen, 'a tree full of angels at Peckham' and 'Ezekiel sitting under a green bough' for which 'lie' he was beaten by his mother.? Wordsworth, in his way, was also a visionary but believed his experience was in some measure universal and that he spoke for all mankind:

> Whether we be young or old
> Our destiny, our being's heart and home,
> Is with infinitude, and only there;
> With hope it is, hope that can never die,
> Effort, and expectation, and desire,
> And something evermore about to be.

Now we cannot perceive infinitude, at least, not with the sensuous eye: when, in the same passage, Wordsworth speaks of 'a flash that has revealed The invisible world' it is not 'the light of sense' but an illumination in the mind he means: neither can we see the immanent spirit of the universe, nor 'unknown modes of being', but we can and do, in some sense, *desire* all of them; indeed human nature seems so constituted that it cannot ultimately desire anything less. That is its triumph and its tragedy. As Carlyle says: 'The misfortune of man has its source in his greatness; for there is something infinite in him and he cannot succeed in burying himself completely in the finite.' Mere worldly, temporal pleasures will always leave the spirit unappeased.

Now it is not always absolutely clear from autobiographical accounts of the unattended moment whether the element of desire or longing, when it is mentioned as present at all, is an integral part of the experience itself, or of its aftermath or sometimes, perhaps, an antecedent feeling which the moment itself assuages briefly. Probably the writer himself is not always clear about this. The most interesting writer who describes desire as a central part of the experience itself is C. S. Lewis. In the early pages of *Surprised by Joy* he recounts three experiences which befell him between the ages of six and eight. They were important, indeed, he says of them: 'In a sense the central story of my life is about nothing else', and he recognizes his difficulty of writing about them. 'The thing has been much better done by Traherne and Wordsworth,' he says, 'but everyman must tell his own tale.' They were experiences of 'joy', 'enormous bliss', but yet nearer to pain than to mere pleasure, for desire is an essential part of them. Here is his account of the first of them.

> The first is itself the memory of a memory. As I stood beside a flowering currant bush on a summer day there suddenly arose in me without warning, and as if from a depth not of years but of centuries, the memory of that earlier morning at the Old House when my brother had brought his toy garden into the nursery. It is difficult to find words strong enough for the sensation which came over me; Milton's 'enormous bliss' of Eden (giving the full, ancient meaning to 'enormous') comes somewhere near it. It was a sensation, of course, of desire; but desire for what? Not, certainly, for a biscuit-tin filled with moss, nor even (though that came into it) for my own past. – And before I knew what I desired, the desire itself was gone, the whole glimpse withdrawn, the world turned commonplace again, or only stirred by a longing for the longing that had just ceased. It had taken only a moment of time; and in a certain sense everything else that had ever happened to me was insignificant by comparison.

The second experience came through reading a Beatrix Potter story and the third from a translation of a Norse poem. He concludes:

> I will only underline the quality common to the three experiences; it is that of an unsatisfied desire which is itself more desirable than any other satisfaction. I call it Joy, which is here a technical term and must be sharply distinguished both from Happiness and from Pleasure. Joy (in my sense) has indeed one characteristic, and one only, in common with them; the fact that anyone who has experienced it will want it again.[1]

78

The experience of 'joy' did not return until the author was in his 'teens, and by then it was again inextricably mixed with nostalgia—*Sehnsucht*—for the earlier childhood experiences. Lewis is unusual, one suspects, in that two of these three experiences came from books rather than from more direct contact with the sensuous world, and the later adolescent experiences were the same in this respect.

Having recognized desire as central to his experiences, Lewis is only one step from asking, 'If the experience is one of desire, what is it that I desire?' and only two steps from 'Whom do I desire?' and finding that 'God' is the answer. These are momentous steps, however, and the second question was not even asked, let alone answered, until he was an adult. The main thread of the book is the story of his spiritual development from these childhood experiences of joy to a full Christian faith. He has written elsewhere: 'If I find in myself a desire which no experience in the world can satisfy, the most probable explanation is that I was made for another world.' The certain hope of that other world enables him to see his childhood experiences, despite the vividness of the memory of them, as mere pale reflections of heavenly truth, a pre-echo of the music of the spheres, and thus to avoid excessive regretful retrospection.

Yvonne Lubbock's experiences also belonged to early childhood but came direct from nature rather than from books. Like C. S. Lewis, she knew herself to belong to eternity and, as with him, her experiences were of the most intense joy and at the same time of great longing scarcely distinguishable from suffering. They had, she believes, a formative influence on her subsequent beliefs. Here is how she describes the first of them.

I was in the garden, muddling about alone. A cuckoo flew over, calling. Suddenly I experienced a sensation that I can only describe as an effect that might follow the rotating of a mental kaleidoscope. It was a feeling of timelessness, not only that time stood still, that duration had ceased, but that I was myself outside time altogether. Somehow I knew that I was part of eternity. And there was also a feeling of spacelessness. I lost all awareness of my surroundings. With this detachment I felt the intensest joy I had ever known, and yet with so great a longing – for what I did not know – that it was scarcely distinguishable from suffering. The only analogous anguish would be that which one experiences in severe physical thirst on the point of being assuaged.

I have no idea how long this experience lasted – I was quite small – but I have never been able entirely to forget it . . .[2]

Her second experience evidently also belonged to childhood, although she says it occurred 'a good while after'. It seems to have been similar to the first, containing 'intensest joy' and 'indescribable longing as of an exile for home', though she says specifically that she felt herself to be in the presence of God. Like many other writers, she came to find, after a period of sceptical agnosticism and intellectual search, an assurance of a world of spirit and spiritual values in the memory of these childhood moments of joy shot through with longing. The ambivalent nature of the experience seems inevitably to prompt the question, 'What do I long for?' The obvious answer – to experience joy again – is, as C. S. Lewis realized, a cul-de-sac because, although joy is infinitely desirable, each experience is itself tinged with desire and prompts the same question and so on *ad infinitum*. Joy as a sensation in one's own mind and body cannot be the answer. To suppose with Richard Jefferies that it is an enlargement of one's own existence one desires is the egotistical trap. And it is a trap; the hook is baited and barbed. So long as one believes one desires a state of one's own consciousness one is hooked on trying ever more extravagant and possibly dangerous expedients to produce that state or one resembling it, whether by the self-flagellation and fasting of some mediaeval hysteric, by alcohol, narcotics or the hallucinogens of the 'beat' generation. 'Beat' is short for the beatific vision to which summit they are always seeking to find short cuts.

Desire points outwards even when the direction is unclear: it cannot be explained or satisfied by being turned in upon itself for its existence and whole character must depend upon the *object* of desire which by definition is no part of the self, the *subject*. We are consciously imperfect and desire perfection, mortal and desire immortality, finite and desire infinitude, as Carlyle said, and so we desire something absolutely 'other', 'out of this world' which Yvonne Lubbock has no difficulty in calling 'God'. Other writers, more sceptical by temperament, perhaps, and lacking what Keats called 'negative capability', have the same experience of desire but by refusing to countenance the possibility of an unknown other dimension are forced by the cul-de-sac back to their starting point in self. This excerpt from A. E. Coppard's autobiography neatly illustrates the circularity of their situation.

> Although I loved my friends and loved to be with them I had a constant yearning for solitude, a desire to go most of my way alone, as though I was instinctively seeking after something still a way out of my reach. What this was, or what it might have been, I didn't know. I didn't care, I didn't bother, I went after it. I still don't know if I ever found it, it may have been sheer idiotic mysticism. Whatever it was, it had no objectivity beyond a craving to shun the familiarities, the nonsense of consciousness and awareness, and simply be; to . . . to . . . commune with something – with whom or what but myself![3]

There is a good deal of evidence, I think, that, however precious solitude, to commune *oneself* is precisely not what satisfies our nameless yearnings. Real or illusory, we long for the experience of perfection and to be taken out of self into a region unconfined by mortality. Great art can speak to our condition: 'I have always believed', says Nicholas Berdyaev in *Dream and Reality*, 'that man's stature and significance is in proportion to that in him which breaks through to infinity. The magic of art is its power to wrench out the roots of finitude and to turn man's gaze to the eternal archetypal forms and images of existence.' But art never wholly satisfies our desire, for it is an appetite which grows with what it feeds on. For some, too, it arouses the desire for emulation. In his fragmentary autobiography, J. M. Synge says of his adolescence:

> I worked myself into a sort of mystical ecstasy with the works of Carlyle and Wordsworth which usually ended by throwing me back into all manner of forebodings. I began to compose and write verses. I wished to be at once Shakespeare, Beethoven and Darwin; my ambition was boundless and a torture to me.

Romantic love with its immortal longings and the discovery of beauty in nature and art are often intertwined, as many writers quoted in earlier chapters have shown, and superlative brief moments of glory may be precipitated at any point. In the same passage quoted above, Synge makes this interesting comment:

> I think the consciousness of beauty is awakened in individuals as in peoples by a prolonged unsatisfied desire. Perhaps the modern feeling for the beauty of nature as a particular quality – an expression of divine ecstasy rather than a mere decoration of the world – arose when men began to look on everything about them with the unsatisfied longing which has its proper analogue in puberty.[4]

Sometimes ethical, aesthetic and erotic impulses may all be combined in an undifferentiated desire as in the following paragraphs from Bruce Frederick Cummings's Journal.

> The day has been overcast, but to-night a soft breeze sprang up and swept the sky clear as softly as a mop. The sun coming out shone upon a white sail far out in the channel, scarcely another vessel hove in sight. The white sail glittered like a piece of silver paper whenever the mainsail swung round as the vessel tacked. Its solitariness and whiteness in a desert of marine blue attracted the attention and held it till at last I could look at nothing else. The sight of it, so clean and white and fair, set me yearning for all the rarest and most exquisite things my imagination could conjure up – a beautiful girl, with fair and sunburnt skin, brown eyes, dark eyebrows, and small pretty feet; a dewdrop in a violet's face; an orange-tip butterfly swinging on an umbel of a flower.
>
> The sail went on twinkling and began to exert an almost moral influence over me. It drew out all the good in me. I longed to follow it on white wings – an angel I suppose – to quit this husk of a body 'as raiment put away', and pursue Truth and Beauty across the sea to the horizon, and beyond the horizon up the sky itself to its last tenuous confines, no doubt with a still small voice summoning me and the rest of the elect to an Agapemone, with Dr Spurgeon at the door distributing tracts.
>
> I can scoff like this now. But at the time my exaltation was very real. My soul strained in the leash. I was full of desire for unattainable spiritual beauty. I wanted something. But I don't know what I want.[5]

The facetious tone which he adopts one also finds in a good deal of poetry by intelligent adolescents. It arises, I think, out of a fear of ridicule, of being misunderstood or of being accused of straining too self-consciously after the divine afflatus. All post-Freudian writers, too, must be aware that they may be revealing more than they intend to a reader with real or imagined psycho-analytic skills.

Ruskin had no such modern fears and was not at all inhibited by considerations of modesty from declaring himself a rare and superior spirit. In *Praeterita* he says: 'I had in my little clay pitcher, vialfuls, as it were, of Wordsworth's reverence, Shelley's sensitiveness, Turner's accuracy, all in one. A snowdrop was to me, as to Wordsworth, part of the Sermon on the Mount.' We have seen Yvonne Lubbock compare the element of longing in her experiences to severe physical thirst. To Ruskin it was 'heart-hunger' that was evoked in him by the simplicity, the severity and the silence of the Wordsworthian landscape.

> Lastly, although there was no definite religious sentiment mingled with it, there was a continual perception of Sanctity in the whole of nature, from the slightest thing to the vastest; an instinctive awe, mixed with delight; an indefinable thrill, such as we sometimes imagine to indicate the presence of a disembodied spirit. I could only feel this perfectly when I was alone; and then it would often make me shiver from head to foot with the joy and fear of it, when after being some time away from hills I first got to the shore of a mountain river, where the brown water circled among the pebbles, or when I first saw the swell of distant land against the sunset, or the first low broken wall, covered with mountain moss. I cannot in the least describe the feeling; but I do not think this is my fault, nor that of the English language, for I am afraid no feeling is describable. If we had to explain even the sense of bodily hunger to a person who had never felt it, we should be hard put to it for words; and the joy in nature seemed to me to come of a sort of heart-hunger, satisfied with the presence of a Great and Holy Spirit.[6]

Ruskin goes on to wonder how many people had experiences in youth like his own and concludes: 'In the same degree they are not of course common, otherwise children would be, most of them, very different from what they are in their choice of pleasures.' It is certainly true that most of the experiences we have been considering occurred in solitude and silence, whereas most children are noisy and gregarious.

9 *The Inner Freedom*

The last chapter was about desire, restlessness, heart-hunger, that element in the unattended moment that is, as Yvonne Lubbock said, like the indescribable longing of an exile for home. Remembering his return to Hawkshead in 1788 for his first long vacation from Cambridge, Wordsworth wrote:

> A comfort seemed to touch
> A heart that had not been disconsolate:
> Strength came where weakness was not known to be,
> At least not felt; and restoration came
> Like an intruder knocking at the door
> Of unacknowledged weariness.

Hawkshead, where he had spent so much of his boyhood, was more truly home to him than his birthplace, Cockermouth. Home is where you can be most truly yourself, where you do not need 'to prepare a face to meet the faces that you meet'. It is, as Robert Frost says, 'Something you somehow haven't to deserve.' To come home, then, particularly to the scenes of childhood, is to experience ease, restoration, one type of inner freedom from the heart-hunger of the exile.

> There is no sense of ease like the ease we felt in those scenes where we were born, where objects became dear to us before we had known the labour of choice, and where the outer world seemed only an extension of our own personality: we accepted and loved it as we accepted our own sense of existence and our own limbs.

So wrote George Eliot. Those scenes of childhood have had an indelible effect on our tastes and attitudes, on what strikes us as true, beautiful and fitting. Whether she is aware of it or not, it is exactly Wordsworth's lesson she is repeating:

> those first affections,
> Those shadowy recollections,
> Which, be they what they may,
> Are yet the fountain-light of all our day,
> Are yet a master light of all our seeing . . .

After reflecting on man's restless striving for something better which we explored in the last chapter, George Eliot continues:

> But heaven knows where that striving might lead us, if our affections had not a trick of twining round those old inferior things – if the loves and sanctities of our life had no deep immovable roots in memory. One's delight in an elderberry bush overhanging the confused leafage of a hedgerow bank, as a more gladdening sight than the finest cistus or fuchsia spreading itself on the softest undulating turf, is an entirely unjustifiable preference to a nursery-gardener, or to any of those severely regulated minds who are free from the weakness of any attachment that does not rest on a demonstrable superiority of qualities. And there is no better reason for preferring this elderberry bush than that it stirs an early memory – that it is no novelty in my life, speaking to me merely through my present sensibilities to form and colour, but the long companion of my existence, that wove itself into my joys when joys were vivid.[1]

It is not all the scenes of childhood indifferently that have a beneficent and restorative power; not any eldertree that remains a gracious memory but a particular one –

> . . . there's a Tree, of many, one,
> A single Field which I have looked upon . . .

– says Wordsworth. Some places like some 'spots of time' are more potent than others, however often we return to them. Thoreau found in Walden Woods 'an infinite and unaccountable friendliness . . . I was so distinctly made aware of something kindred to me even in scenes which we are accustomed to call wild and dreary . . . that I thought no place could ever be strange to me again.' Forrest Reid found another of these 'good' places, the graveyard of a ruined church, when he was a child in Ireland.

> I had chanced on this graveyard quite unexpectedly one morning when out for a walk. The season was spring, but a spell of summer seemed to have fallen on this place: the winds were hushed, the air mild and caressing. And as I sat on a sun-warmed, fallen head-stone, I felt that I had wandered into the very heart of Peace. Thrushes and rooks and starlings flitted about the church tower, while directly in front of me was a mass of flaming crimson blossom, where a flowering currant had found a roothold among the crumbling stones. I know not what there was about this place that so entranced me. It was a beauty that seemed mingled with innocence and simplicity; it had a definitely *moral* quality, which dropped

deep down into my soul and made me feel good. I very seldom felt good. I very seldom *was* good, though I loved goodness in other people. But as I sat in that churchyard all my restless thoughts and impulses sank away: I was like one of Wordsworth's little boys or little girls, and could have held a dialogue with the sage precisely in their manner had his mild old ghost come woolgathering by . . .[2]

The place was beautiful and made him feel good but who shall say what beauty and goodness are? Did his eye make the churchyard beautiful or the churchyard make him good? Because the unattended moment is unitive it heals these harmful dualisms into which the speculative mind of man for ever tends to polarize the wholeness of experience. Both the object and the subject were compounded of innocence, which is freedom from association with guilt and sin, simplicity which is freedom from confusion and complexity, peace which is freedom from noise and from restless thoughts and impulses. And even place and time become confounded. It was one elder tree, a single field, a particular churchyard, none of them, perhaps, special in themselves except that each must have been seen with the eye of vision in one of those special moments in and out of time which gave them ever after a particular power to free the mind, to lighten 'the burthen of the mystery', to give authentic tidings of 'central peace, subsisting at the heart of endless agitation'.

> There are in our existence spots of time,
> Which with distinct pre-eminence retain
> A vivifying virtue, whence, depressed
> By false opinion and contentious thought,
> Or aught of heavier or more deadly weight,
> In trivial occupations, and the round
> Of ordinary intercourse, our minds
> Are nourished and invisibly repaired;
> A virtue, by which pleasure is enhanced,
> That penetrates, enables us to mount,
> When high, more high, and lifts us up when fallen.
>
> Such moments, worthy of all gratitude,
> Are scattered everywhere, taking their date
> From our first childhood: in our childhood even
> Perhaps are most conspicuous.[3]

We have already seen how Richard Church could say about the childhood experience with which chapter 7 began that it lit 'a fire within me, lightening my mind'. We have also heard Margiad Evans exclaim: 'My heart is *freed* by the memories of those first joyous pains . . . renewing my being, filling my breast like a fountain, opening my eyes.' It is little wonder, then, that the unattended moment may be seen as somehow analogous to a conversion. William James defined religious conversion as 'the process, gradual or sudden, by which a self hitherto divided, and consciously wrong, inferior and un-happy, becomes unified and consciously right, superior and happy, in consequence of its firmer hold upon religious realities'. The differences are two-fold: renovation need not come to the *consciously* disconsolate but more likely as 'Strength . . . where weakness was not known to be'; and religion in any ordinary sense need not be involved. It all depends, perhaps, what we mean by religious *realities*. Quiller-Couch's childish fears of hell fire and divine retribution for wrong doing were real enough and, as we saw in chapter 2, it was a moment caught in a shaft of sunlight in Bradley Wood which finally chased away those religious terrors which had beset him so balefully. Certainly there are examples in plenty of intense moments with their attendant surge of feeling sweeping away belief in dead ritual and creed. There are examples in other chapters, notably from Mark Rutherford, Edmund Gosse, A. L. Rowse and C. S. Lewis, but here we will only look at two paragraphs from Morag Coate.

I was alone in my attic lodging when the moment came. I reviewed once again the main outlines of the Christian dogma. I said at last firmly and clearly to myself, 'I do not know if any of these things are true, and I see no possible way of finding out.' I sat still, as though waiting for a doom to fall, expecting that I would find myself somehow thrust out into the darkness of night. Instead I became totally at peace. A tall plane tree spread its wide leaves and dangled the miniature worlds of its round seed vessels outside my window. I looked at it, and found there the outer loveliness of the truth which was spreading into me. Beauty existed as a part of life; life was a natural aspect of unforced reality, and I was part of it. A sense of liberation, almost of rebirth, came to me. I was myself at last.

The experience was astonishing only because it was so new; the naturalness of it carried a profound reassurance. At the moment of losing belief, faith flowed into me; a deep and lasting, comprehensive faith in life. From that moment onwards the thought

87

of death no longer troubled me. I was a part of the life stream and would sink back into it when my separate life was ended. Beauty and truth would still remain; others would share and carry forward my own standards after I was gone. The concept of a personal God was no part of my own experience, and I dismissed it from then on. I felt no loss in that, only a tremendous gain in courage and vitality and hope.[4]

The thought of death, she says, no longer troubled her. If we are haunted by the fear of death or hell-fire, then to be freed from those obsessions is the greatest imaginable liberation. Stone walls do not a prison make nor iron bars a cage because whether or not we *feel* free subjectively may be more important than the objective freedom we actually enjoy. Hamlet said he could be bounded in a nut shell and count himself king of infinite space were it not that he had bad dreams. The unattended moment, it seems, with its sense of timelessness, is often understood to contain not intimations only but an absolute assurance of immortality which dispells bad dreams of death. Tennyson knew that 'death was an almost laughable impossibility' and R. M. Bucke did not merely come to believe but *saw* that 'the soul of man is immortal'. Edward Carpenter, in 1883 (the same year as Jefferies' *The Story of My Heart*), published a volume of Whitmanesque free verse somewhat mysteriously entitled *Towards Democracy*. In a note appended to some of the later editions of the book he describes the exalted state of mind in which the poems had been poured out in 1881.

I became for the time overwhelmingly conscious of the disclosure within of a region transcending in some sense the ordinary bounds of personality, in the light of which region my own idiosyncrasies of character – defects, accomplishments, limitations, or what not – appeared of no importance whatever – *an absolute freedom from mortality*, accompanied by an indescribable calm and joy . . .

Inner freedom, subjective freedom, depends on an equilibrium between what we desire and our ability to satisfy that desire. Always there are two ways of maintaining that balance. One is to increase our power of satisfying our wants – getting and spending, acquiring more power, more status and what, ironically, we call more 'goods': this is the track on which our affluent consumer society seems to be set with an accelerating

momentum which constantly frustrates the search for freedom because our competitive and clamorous wants know no
limit: 'the world moves in appetency, on its metalled ways'.
'O fools,' said the Silurist Henry Vaughan from his retreat in
the Breconshire mountains, 'thus to prefer dark night Before
true light.' Two centuries before Wordsworth, he had

> ... felt through all this fleshly dresse
> Bright shootes of everlastingness.

The other way to inner freedom is Vaughan's way, to
reduce our wants, to be satisfied with less, to discover again
the simplicity of the basic needs which we share with all
creatures, the way of Thoreau in Walden Woods. It is the path
of the mystic, the hermit, the recluse and sometimes, today
hopefully, of the hippy and the drop-out. It is a path that has
been better understood and more frequently trodden in the
East than in the West. Rabindranath Tagore, though by no
means a hermit, always retained a feeling for the elemental
simplicities of village life in his native Bengal. Much of his life
was spent in trying to reconcile the philosophy and religion
of East and West. As a young man he had an experience which
was important in giving direction to his life, freeing him from
confusion, uniting the unmeaning fragments of experience:
the coming of the monsoon rains quenching drought were the
outward symbol for the beginning of an inner freedom from
thirst for coherence.

When I grew older and was employed in a responsible work in some
villages I took my place in a neighbourhood where the current of
time ran slow and joys and sorrows had their simple and elemental shades and lights. The day which had its special significance
for me came with all its drifting trivialities of the commonplace
life. The ordinary work of my morning had come to its close, and
before going to take my bath I stood for a moment at my window,
overlooking a market-place on the bank of a dry river bed, wel-
coming the first flood of rain along its channel. Suddenly I became
conscious of a stirring of soul within me. My world of experience
in a moment seemed to be lighted, the facts that were detached and
dim found a great unity of meaning. The feeling which I had was
like that which a man, groping through a fog without knowing
his destination, might feel when he suddenly discovers that he
stands before his own house.
    ... All things that had seemed like vagrant waves were revealed

to my mind in relation to a boundless sea. I felt sure that some Being who comprehended me and my world was seeking his best expression in all my experiences, uniting them into an ever widening individuality which is a spiritual work of art . . . I felt that I had found my religion at last, the religion of Man, in which the infinite became defined in humanity and came close to me so as to need my love and co-operation.[5]

To love mankind without reservation, as Tagore conspicuously did, is to love without desire. It is the occupation of a saint. But love in our language is *eros* as well as *agape*. To desire is not to be free but a prisoner and sexual desire is, for many, one of the strongest, most captivating desires and its gratification, at its best, a glorious, healing liberation. It is hardly surprising, then, that the unattended moment has its orgasmic analogue – sometimes veiled, as we have seen, at other times more nearly explicit.

> Only for a moment; but it was enough. It was a sudden revelation, a tinge like a blush which one tried to check and then, as it spread, one yielded to its expansion, and rushed to the farthest verge and there quivered and felt the world come closer, swollen with some astonishing significance, some pressure of rapture, which split its thin skin and gushed and poured with an extraordinary alleviation over the cracks and sores. Then, for that moment, she had seen an illumination; a match burning in a crocus; an inner meaning almost expressed. But the close withdrew; the hard softened. It was over – the moment.[6]

This is from a novel, but can anyone doubt that there is a great deal of autobiography in all Virginia Woolf's novels and that there is something of both the daring, impulsive, cigarette-smoking Sally Seton and the rather timid, slightly chilly Clarissa Dalloway in her own character? In 1918 she wrote for *The Times Literary Supplement* an essay called *Moments of Vision* in which she says: 'Such moments of vision are of an unaccountable nature; leave them alone and they persist for years; try to explain them and they disappear; write them down and they die beneath the pen.' It would be very easy to quote here two other novelists among her contemporaries where fiction and autobiography imperceptibly merge; James Joyce, who called moments of vision 'epiphanies' in *Stephen Hero* and D. H. Lawrence, who often ascribes a quasi-mystical significance to sexual union.

Finally in this chapter let us return to Hugh Fausset about the psychological wretchedness of whose boyhood we said something in chapter 5. He had an unforgettable experience in the summer of 1914 between leaving school and going up to Cambridge. He had climbed to a Pennine fell top and watched twilight fade into night.

> I knew the happiness of a peace so perfect that nothing, it seemed, could ever disturb it. And perhaps for the first time I realised consciously the delusion involved in all the hungry quest of personal happiness. The happiness of this eternal moment was given to me because I had momentarily surrendered every nervous claim upon life. I had not willed it, but received it as a divine gift of some divine will.
>
> This peace that passed understanding, this joy that was like a tide of music flowing with a calm compulsion and from an infinite source through my whole being was the reality at the heart of life. And the only necessary aim in human life was to qualify to receive and express it, to prepare the self like a bride for the coming of the bridegroom, to make of the body and mind a temple of the Holy Ghost.
>
> For the first time in my life something of the eternal meaning which underlay all the unreality of religious creeds and factions dawned upon me. There was a necessary relation between the spirit that animated the secret places of the earth and the vast circumference of the sky and hill and the words which I had so often unwittingly heard and glibly repeated in church and chapel – 'O Lord, make clean our hearts within us, and take not Thy Holy Spirit from us'.[7]

10 Words Move, Music Moves

Words and music *move* in two senses; T. S. Eliot several times exploits the ambiguity of the word. A musical work moves through the time it takes to perform or listen to it from the first bar to the last; a poem or novel similarly has to be read from the opening to the closing words. Only when the temporal dimension is transcended, when we know the work so well that we can contemplate it whole in our minds, can it truly move in the second sense: then it is still but it moves most deeply; like a Chinese jar or a Grecian urn it still moves perpetually in its stillness. So the perfect work of art perfectly comprehended achieves something of the stillness of eternity. This is a rare beatitude.

One of Eliot's preoccupations in the *Four Quartets* is with those moments when our ordinary experience in the temporal flow is interrupted by more fragmentary epiphanies or manifestations of a timeless 'real' world. Most of us do not attend to these elusive and momentary intersections of the timeless with time because we do not recognize or cannot hold on to their significance; we are too accustomed to our familiar dimension of past and future. Such moments for Eliot, we may suppose, were associated with the rose garden of Burnt Norton and with a mid-winter visit to Little Gidding, with an arbour where the rain beat and a draughty church at smokefall, with wild thyme unseen and with winter lightning, as well as with certain combinations of words, certain rhythms and melodies.

Every man could list his own epiphanies if he was attentive to those puzzling moments that do not quite fit into the ordinary pattern of experience. In this chapter we will look at moments which seem to have been precipitated by words or music and, in the first example, both played their part. When Cyril Connolly was at his preparatory school, gramophone records were played to the boys on Saturday evenings. When they came to 'I have a song to sing O', he would open a book he had bought in the Charing Cross Road and read a passage (which he quotes) about a sea bird's 'high carnival over the waste of grey waters'.

The combination of the music with this passage was intoxicating. The two blended into an experience of isolation and flight which induced the sacred shiver. The classroom disappeared, I was alone on the dark seas, there was a hush, a religious moment of suspense, and the Manx shearwaters appeared, held their high carnival, etc., and vanished. Then, the schoolroom where each boy sat by his desk, his few possessions inside, his charted ink channels on top, returned to focus. This experience, which I repeated like a drug every Saturday, was typical of the period; for those were the days when literature meant the romantic escape, the purple passage . . .[1]

Cyril Connolly's experience is, perhaps, unusual in that, given the appropriate stimulus, he could repeat it at regular intervals. It is interesting to note how a complex of religious and aesthetic assumptions about the experience which the words and music induced are implied by the way he describes it: it was 'intoxicating', it induced the 'sacred shiver' and a 'religious moment of suspense', yet was clearly part of his dawning artistic sensibility. The experience also had a trance-like quality in that he was 'transported', lost to the school-room world, oblivious, briefly, of his surroundings.

The same quality of 'transport' characterizes an experience which happened to C. S. Lewis at the age of fourteen or fifteen and left him, in a school-room too, 'like a man recovering from unconsciousness'. He had known unattended moments in earlier childhood, as we saw in chapter 8, but the intervening years at boarding school which he calls 'the Concentration Camp' had been 'Dark Ages' about which he says: 'The authentic "Joy" had vanished from my life; so completely that not even the memory of the desire of it remained.' And then came the moment of its return, utterly unheralded and unanticipated. He happened to see, in some literary periodical, the title *Siegfried and the Twilight of the Gods* and one of Arthur Rackham's illustrations when suddenly . . .

> Pure 'Northernness' engulfed me: a vision of huge, clear spaces hanging above the Atlantic in the endless twilight of Northern summer, remoteness, severity . . . and almost at the same moment I knew that I had met this before, long, long ago . . . And with that plunge back into my own past there arose at once, almost like heart-break, the memory of Joy itself, the knowledge that I had once had what I had now lacked for years.[2]

C. S. Lewis's experience, which he calls an unendurable sense of desire and loss, was touched off by words and an Arthur Rackham picture. Gavin Maxwell had an experience which was triggered by another illustration combined with the shock of a minor accident. Though neither music nor words were involved, his account must be included here because of its close similarity to Lewis's vision of 'pure Northernness' coupled with intense longing. Gavin Maxwell, ten years old and also at boarding school, had cut his hand deeply.

> I went upstairs to Matron's room, and while I was waiting for her to find a dressing I entered a dream that remained with me for many years. On the table was some boy's picture-book, and on the cover was a garishly painted polar landscape. In the foreground a polar bear stood heraldic on an ice-floe; the sea around it was deep blue, fathomless with secrets, and across the vast background of ink-blue sky flamed a stupendous curtain of multi-coloured aurora borealis. I was drawn into a majesty of icy desolation and loneliness, of limitless space and aweful splendour, colder and remoter than the stars, so that my throat tightened and I wanted to cry because it was so beautiful and terrible. There were tears in my eyes when Matron came back and she thought it was because of the pain in my hand. The longing stayed with me, and when I first travelled alone, fourteen years later, it was to the arctic that I journeyed.[3]

It is curious, perhaps, that the words, the music, the pictures which triggered these three experiences were not in themselves very remarkable; a garish picture in a boy's book, an Arthur Rackham drawing, a song from Gilbert & Sullivan, a passage about the behaviour of a sea bird and so forth. And yet an experience which makes a man, many years later, travel to the arctic, is not unremarkable. It seems that the words or picture or music may move in the sense of *precipitating* the experience, but they do not necessarily *cause* it. Relatively objective factors such as the kind of picture, the quality of the music may be less important than subjective ones such as the state of the person prior to the experience, his readiness for it. At least there would seem to be some chance conjunction between a subjective state and an object which acts as a catalyst.

This is certainly true of Richard Church. We have already seen how the opening words of St John's Gospel casually glimpsed in his school Bible at the age of eleven made the hair on his head tingle, a red curtain of blood fall before his eyes while the world rocked around him. Some five years later on a November day, Richard Church was again precipitated by some words into an experience of life-changing consequence. It came after nearly a year of 'spiritual dolour'. He was facing a dark and uncertain future, in a mood of 'rebellious anarchy' and frustrated of any means of self-expression. He had been obliged to relinquish a scholarship at an art school for a clerical job in the city by day and nursing his dying mother by night. One morning he was standing by the bedside of his brother with whom he shared this task and who was also ill on this occasion. Outside the window, council workmen could be heard cutting down some beloved aspen trees in advance of the jerry builders who were transforming the semi-rural character of the suburb in which they lived. Casually he picked up a copy of Keats from his brother's quilt. 'I opened the book of poems, and idly began to read the verses beginning "I stood tiptoe upon a little hill". . . . What followed,' he says, 'is impossible to describe.' However, forty years later in an introduction to a selection of Keats's poems he did try to describe it. Here is the passage:

> I recollect still a physical cataclysm that came upon me. A great flash of light blinded my eyes; a sense of something opening, as it were a parting of clouds. I found that I too was standing tiptoe, staring up the hill in a sort of agony of attention, trying to absorb something that had happened to me. The sound of the aspens, like surf on shingle, came sighing into my flung-open soul and it was too much for me. I turned to my brother in my distress, to find him looking at me curiously, but with an understanding that made the ordeal more tolerable. The dreadful loneliness of it was shared. Neither of us said anything. We even looked away from each other shyly. After a pause, I asked him if I might borrow the book, and he agreed almost gruffly. That was for me the beginning of my life in the world of poetry, the world which is the sunward side, the very reality of our everyday life.[4]

It is little wonder that Richard Church says his experience gave him an abiding sense of having been selected for some particular destiny or that he describes it as a 'Pauline encounter'. To find one's artistic vocation so suddenly and certainly is bound to invite comparison with the more dramatic kind of religious conversion. In its physical manifestations, Paul's experience has often been likened to some kind of epileptic episode and the same may be said of Richard Church's case, though to say this is in no way to belittle the importance of the experience or its consequences.

Another writer who seriously compares the effect of some poetry on him to Paul's encounter on the Damascus road is William Hale White under his pseudonym 'Mark Rutherford'. He had been two years at theological college, his heart altogether untouched, he says, by anything he had heard or read when he chanced on the *Lyrical Ballads*. It was a revelation: all his natural pent up reverence was transferred to Wordsworth's God of nature.

> Instead of an object of worship which was altogether artificial, remote, never coming into genuine contact with me, I had now one which I thought to be real, one in which literally I could live and move and have my being, an actual fact present before my eyes. God was brought from that heaven of the books, and resided on the downs visible in the far-away distances seen from the top of a hill and in every cloud shadow which wandered across the valley. Wordsworth unconsciously did for me what every religious reformer has done – he re-created my Supreme Divinity, substituting a new and living spirit for the old deity, once alive but gradually hardened into an idol.[5]

Autobiographical testimony to the effect of Wordsworth's poetry would deserve a volume to itself but this example, together with an even better known one from John Stuart Mill's autobiography, are among the most interesting. White's experience can only be called a conversion, even – without unduly straining the meaning of words – a *religious* conversion, and yet it turned him away from his intention of becoming a dissenting minister to a career of modest distinction as civil servant and man of letters sustained, in private, by a secular natural piety of a Wordsworthian kind.

In passing, it is interesting to notice that many of Wordsworth's poems which had such a disturbing but ultimately life-enhancing effect on his readers were themselves inspired by words. It was the words of Dorothy's journal about a butterfly or a sparrow's nest or a belt of daffodils 'the breadth of a country turnpike road' beside Ullswater that moved her brother to composition, though in the last case they reminded him of a shared experience. His famous lyric 'To a Solitary Reaper' was suggested by a passage in Thomas Wilkinson's *Tour of the Highlands* rather than by any particular incident on his own tour with Dorothy and Coleridge in the summer of 1803. The sentence that particularly moved him reads: 'Passed a female, who was reaping alone: she sung in Erse, as she bended over her sickle; the sweetest human voice I ever heard: her strains were tenderly melancholy, and felt delicious long after they were heard no more.' Words after speech and the memory of music reach into the silence. Rilke would declare in Orphic exaltation that only in song was true existence to be found.

Words move, words and music together move in the song of a Hebridean girl, or music alone may be

> . . . heard so deeply
> That it is not heard at all, but you are the music
> While the music lasts.

A. F. Webling, like Richard Church, was a poor young clerk in London, working in an office by day and studying for examinations at night. His one escape and recreation was to visit city churches to listen to the music.

> On one occasion, when listening to a certain passage of music which seemed to me of more than earthly beauty, I chanced to look up at a picture of the Transfiguration. I saw it with half-closed eyes. The scene around me faded. The music seemed to die away, and for a moment my spirit was caught up into a place of eternal calm. This state of perfect tranquility, combined with full consciousness, passed in a flash, and the silver chiming of the sanctus bell brought me back to earth. But I learned at that moment just enough to feel that while man remains man, retaining his mysterious intuitions of things that lie beyond, so long will the Mass afford to hearts attuned to its significance the most precious link between earth and heaven.[6]

The author of this passage might well have been the prototype of Leonard Bast in *Howards End*, the young clerk who read Ruskin and attended Queen's Hall concerts for self-improvement. It is easy for the waspish Mr Forster to be satirical at his expense: '. . . he hoped to come to Culture suddenly, much as the Revivalist hopes to come to Jesus . . . He believed in sudden conversion, a belief which may be right, but which is peculiarly attractive to a half-baked mind. It is the basis of much popular religion.' Benedick in *Much Ado about Nothing* was jesting, too, when he exclaimed, 'Is it not strange that sheep's guts should hale souls out of men's bodies?' In sober fact, however, the evidence, inconvenient though it may be to the sceptic, is overwhelming, of the power of music not merely to soothe the troubled breast or stir to martial valour but to precipitate experiences which are ecstatic in the strictest sense of the word.

Warner Allen provides a good example which, by coincidence, also occurred at the Queen's Hall. He describes himself on the threshold of fifty as 'hostile to the apparent sloppiness of fashionable mysticism' and quite content to regard the meaning of the universe as shrouded in impenetrable darkness. Then a peculiarly vivid dream (which he does not describe) led him to review his own past life hoping to trace 'some pattern and design that underlay its outward incoherence'. The answer came during a performance of Beethoven's Seventh Symphony; it 'slipped into the interval between two demi-semi-quavers of the triumphant fast movement.'

> Rapt in Beethoven's music, I closed my eyes and watched a silver glow which shaped itself into a circle with a central focus brighter than the rest. The circle became a tunnel of light proceeding from some distant sun in the heart of the Self. Swiftly and smoothly I was borne through the tunnel and as I went the light turned from silver to gold. There was an impression of drawing strength from a limitless sea of power and a sense of deepening peace. The light grew brighter, but was never dazzling or alarming. I came to a point where time and motion ceased. In my recollection it took the shape of a flat-topped rock, surrounded by a summer sea, with a sandy pool at its foot. The dream scene vanished and I am absorbed in the Light of the universe, in Reality glowing like fire with the knowledge of itself, without ceasing to be one and myself, merged like a drop of quick-silver in the Whole, yet still separate as a grain of sand in the desert. The peace that passes all understanding and the pulsating energy of creation are one in the centre in the midst of conditions where all opposites are reconciled.[7]

Once again an experience, not just of perfect peace but a conviction of having been united with another order of reality, slipped into the timeless moment between two notes of Beethoven's music: he was then, in Eliot's words, 'surrounded by a grace of sense, a white light still and moving'. The author's account of the experience, as he freely admits, is coloured by his subsequent reading of St Teresa and other religious mystical writings. Warner Allen's experience was received by him as the answer to a problem with which he had been wrestling for some time: it gave him access to a system of belief which, without it, would have continued to seem incredible. It was almost, one might say, the missing foundation stone for a temple he had been building in the air.

Warner Allen was a middle-aged man seeking for meaning and purpose in his life, typical, perhaps, of those people in the second half of life whose problems, Jung says, are spiritual rather than psychological, and who can never be fully healed without finding or regaining a religious outlook on life. Basil Willey was a dejected and somewhat neurotic adolescent. Here is how he describes himself.

> I was always, as I have said, 'in pursuit of something' – and I can think of no better words for it than 'joy', 'blessedness', or 'felicity'; it was certainly not 'pleasure' in the ordinary sense of that word, nor even 'happiness'. It was a heightened state of being, an intensified sense of life; it was, I suppose, what every romantic has always sought. For me it meant, in particular, escape from the banalities and monotonies of suburbia, and release from the dejection and the morbid anxieties which beset my lonely and not-very-childish childhood. It was this quest that determined my tastes and pursuits: reading, music, architecture, botany, geology and landscape . . .

The same symphony of Beethoven was implicated in bringing to his misery and anxiety a relief, reassurance and peace similar to Warner Allen's even if it was experienced more on the emotional plane and did not, at the time, have the same metaphysical implications.

> One day, when my sufferings were at their worst, I was listening to the Seventh Symphony, and suddenly, as the wood-wind announced the lovely, tranquil theme of the Trio to the Scherzo, I felt the load drop from me, as Bunyan's pilgrim did before the Cross. 'Fear no more', said the Trio; 'fear no more! Underneath are the everlasting arms.' The relief and the reassurance were deep and sweet; and, although the cure had only begun, its power increased steadily. From that moment I could always recapture the renovating virtue by thinking of that Trio.[8]

It is interesting to note that Willey borrows Wordsworth's phrase 'renovating virtue' from the same passage in the Twelfth Book of *The Prelude* as his title *Spots of Time*. There are other impressive examples in the book of music's power to move, but there is not space to quote them here.

What the murmuring shell of time murmurs to those who attend is the injunction that 'You shall not think "the past is finished" ', not your own past, nor that of mankind, nor even of the old earth herself. Many times we have seen how the unattended moment, recalled to mind, annihilates the intervening years. This is within the lifetime of one man only which, *sub specie aeternitatis*, is no more than the blink of an eye-lid – 'his days are as a shadow that passeth away'. But there is a species of experience well documented in which a man may seem to be united momentarily not with some portion of his own past but with a distant period of history or, indeed, with the whole vast panorama of recorded time.

The historian, of course, habitually tries to see events in this perspective: in *Signs of the Times*, Carlyle says, 'The poorest day that passes over us is the conflux of two eternities; it is made up of the currents that issue from the remotest Past, and flow onwards to the remotest Future.' If our poorest days are such a conflux, by contrast our finest and most memorable – or so the evidence of this book suggests – are those containing moments which detach themselves from this flux of time: then the conflux of time past and time future becomes a moment of timeless Now. Without such moments we should be, in Eliot's metaphor, helpless detritus tossed along in a strong brown river: we should be travelling, back-to-the-engine and destination unknown, on a single track railway. The past lies all before us, the journey we have already travelled, but if we lean out of the carriage to see where the train is going, we shall get a crick in the neck of the mind, so to speak, and be blinded by smoke and cinders in the wind.

Carlyle saw the building of the railways but he was by no means complacent, as most of his contemporaries were, about the direction of man's material progress. Though he rejected most of the religious doctrines on which he had been reared he remained a true Calvinist in ceaselessly chastizing the follies of his own backsliding generation. But despite the unorthodoxy of his religious beliefs and his chronic dyspepsia, he was sustained as an historian by some faith that in the unfolding of history a mysterious but nevertheless divine purpose would ultimately be fulfilled. Without such a faith, history is a tale told by an idiot, a purgatory with no promise of heaven beyond. Voltaire said it was nothing but a pack of tricks we play upon the dead and another sceptic of the age of reason, Edward Gibbon, as everybody knows, called it little more than a record of the crimes, follies and misfortunes of mankind.

It is interesting that the author of the *Decline and Fall*, ordinarily so critical and restrained, had experienced more romantic emotions of some intensity. About his first visit to Rome he wrote:

> My temper is not very susceptible of enthusiasm, and the enthusiasm which I do not feel I have ever scorned to affect. But at the distance of twenty-five years I can neither forget nor express the strong emotions which agitated my mind as I first approached and entered the *eternal city*. After a sleepless night, I trod, with a lofty step, the ruins of the Forum; each memorable spot where Romulus *stood*, or Tully spoke, or Caesar fell, was at once present to my eye; and the several days of intoxication were lost or enjoyed before I could descend to a cool and minute investigation.

So for a few days Gibbon was filled with a warm glow of imaginative excitement most uncharacteristic of his Augustan temperament – a few days which were '*lost or enjoyed*'; what a telling phrase! Compared with his subsequent years of scholarly toil, they may have seemed idle days, but Wordsworth could have told him that the things ultimately of greatest importance in our lives often occur 'even in what seem our most unfruitful hours'. How could Gibbon, even for a moment, have thought of those days as 'lost' in which the idea for his life's work was conceived?

> It was at Rome, on the 15th of October 1764, as I sat musing amidst the ruins of the Capitol, while the barefooted friars were singing vespers in the temple of Jupiter, that the idea of writing the decline and fall of the city first started to my mind.[1]

Richard Jefferies was not a historian nor ever in Rome except in imagination and his temper was somewhat more given to what Gibbon would have called 'enthusiasm'.

. . . I went to Pevensey, and immediately the ancient wall swept my mind back seventeen hundred years to the eagle, the pilum, and the short sword. The grey stones, the thin red bricks laid by those whose eyes had seen Caesar's Rome, lifted me out of the grasp of house-life, of modern civilisation, of those minutiae which occupy the moment. The grey stone made me feel as if I had existed from then till now, so strongly did I enter into and see my own life as if reflected. My own existence was focussed back on me; I saw its joy, its unhappiness, its birth, its death, its possibilities among the infinite, above all its yearning Question. Why? Seeing it thus clearly, and lifted out of the moment by the force of seventeen centuries, I recognised the full mystery and the depths of things in the roots of the dry grass on the wall, in the green sea flowing near. Is there anything I can do? The mystery and the possibilities are not in the roots of the grass, nor is the depth of things in the sea; they are in my existence, in my soul. The marvel of existence, almost the terror of it, was flung on me with crushing force by the sea, the sun shining, the distant hills. With all their ponderous weight they made me feel myself: all the time, all the centuries made me feel myself this moment a hundredfold.[2]

The sight of ancient walls sweeps him out of the dimension of quotidian preoccupations which he calls 'the grasp of house life' – a favourite expression of his – into a wider vision. He was often under the shadow of the Yew Tree and obsessed with the Why of existence. On this occasion what Cicero called 'the power of admonition that is in places' jerked his own tormented existence into a more distant and balanced focus with life-enhancing effect. It is not that he forgot himself; rather he was made to 'feel myself this moment a hundredfold'. Most of us probably use the past and the places associated with it in this egocentric way. 'Is it nature', asks Montaigne, 'or by some error of fantasy, that the seeing of places that we know to have been frequented or inhabited by men whose memory is esteemed or mentioned in stories doth in some sort move and stir us up as much or more than hearing their noble deeds?'

This romantic emotion, which must be all but universally felt, can be exploited commercially to sell almost anything from a package tour to a postcard; it can be induced to rouse patriotism or heighten piety; it may be sentimentalized so that it saps the strength of any real care for or curiosity about the past. Undoubtedly it would be a dangerous emotion if overindulged by a historian but it is likely that every great historian's labours have been quickened by some such sense of the past. It was the reading of Sir Walter Scott's novels in boyhood that first turned von Ranke's huge energies to the study of history, as he generously acknowledges, at the same time deploring the historical inaccuracies of parts of *Quentin Durwood*. For C. V. Wedgwood, 'Nothing seems to bridge the gap of the years so much as the unfolding and reading of ancient letters; sometimes minute particles of sand which had long inhered in some thick down stroke where the ink had been wet, detach themselves after three hundred years to blow away and join with yesterday's dust.'[3] It is a feeling, she acknowledges, indefensible in reason and yet she can echo with approval Dr Johnson's sentiment: 'Far from me and from my friends be such frigid philosophy as may conduct us indifferent and unmoved over any ground which has been dignified by wisdom, bravery or virtue. That man is little to be envied whose patriotism would not gain force upon the plain of Marathon or whose piety would not grow warmer among the ruins of Iona.' It was, of course, the remains of St Columba's monastery on the island of Iona, which he visited on his tour of the Hebrides with Boswell, that drew from Johnson this remark. It is good to see from these examples that a 'frigid philosophy' and a hard heart are not the necessary concomitants of a clear head. A feeling for the past as well as accurate scholarship is necessary for the historian who is to animate the great dust heap of history. We might almost say, with Arnold's Scholar Gipsy, 'it needs heaven-sent moments for this skill'.

Like Carlyle, most historians of the past have been sustained either by some faith in a divine purpose being obscurely worked out in human history or by a belief in progress and the perfectibility of man and his societies. Such a belief in the meaningfulness of man's being-in-time is today explicitly or implicitly rejected by most of their successors, which makes Arnold Toynbee a lonely if not a lone figure. Not only does he clearly have a feeling, rising at times to awe, for the poetry in the facts of history but also intimations of a potentially transcendent historical purpose. He uses, not carelessly, a metaphor like mankind scaling a perilous mountain with its implication that however many mountaineers have fallen and perished in the ascent – however many civilizations have flourished and decayed – the possibility of reaching the summit is not outside the bounds of possibility and the urge to reach it is an indubitable fact of human nature. His feeling for the past, furthermore, has sometimes coalesced into an experience of being transported back in time not merely in imagination or reverie but – however nonsensical it seems to say it – in very truth.

A tenuous long-distance commerce exclusively on the intellectual plane is an historian's normal relation to the objects of his study; yet there are moments in his mental life – moments as memorable as they are rare – in which temporal and spatial barriers fall and psychic distance is annihilated; and in such moments of inspiration the historian finds himself transformed in a flash from a remote spectator into an immediate participant, as the dry bones take flesh and quicken into life.

He likens these moments when the intervening centuries are annihilated to an aeroplane's sudden deep drop when it falls into an air pocket. He describes six such moments each associated with his visit to a specific place with powerful historical associations but he had 'a larger and stranger experience' in entirely familiar and humdrum surroundings.

In London in the southern section of the Buckingham Palace Road, walking southwards along the pavement skirting the west wall of Victoria Station, the writer, once, one afternoon not long after the end of the First World War – he has failed to record the exact date – had found himself in communion, not just with this or that episode in History, but with all that had been, and was, and was to come. In that instant he was directly aware of the passage of History gently flowing through him in a mighty current, and of his own life welling like a wave in the flow of this vast tide. The experience lasted long enough for him to take visual note of the Edwardian red brick surface and white stone facings of the station wall gliding past him on his left, and to wonder – half amazed and half amused – why this incongruously prosaic scene should have been the physical setting of a mental illumination. An instant later, the communion had ceased, and the dreamer was back again in the every-day cockney world which was his native social milieu and of which the Edwardian station wall was a characteristic period piece.[4]

As Toynbee recognizes, he has described two rather different kinds of experience. The less rare (though by no means common) type is an inspiration, a spasm of the imagination, perhaps, which provides 'a momentary communion with the actors in a particular historic event'. Our common sense tells us that this must be an illusion but one of such vividness that even a tough-minded scholar to whom it occurs can only describe it as though it were a real suspension of natural laws. Perhaps it only happens to the scholar or person who has absorbed in detail all the historical records of the place he is visiting. It seems analogous in some respects to the moment of scientific discovery when the researcher who has long pondered a problem sees with the suddenness of revelation all the facts fit together as a new coherent picture.

A seeming contradiction of this suggestion is the celebrated strange tale of the Misses Moberley and Jourdain. For part of a hot summer's afternoon in 1901 at the Petit Trianon at Versailles the two ladies apparently independently witnessed scenes associated with Marie Antoinette's tragic last days there. They wrote about it in *An Adventure*.[5] It may, perhaps, have suggested to Henry James the strange subject of his last unfinished novel, *The Sense of the Past*, at which he worked in his declining years to distract his mind from the unimaginable horrors of the first World War. At all events it was a case which provoked much speculation and investigation among psychical researchers in the early years of this century partly because the ladies described non-existent features of the Versailles grounds which were subsequently shown to have existed in the 1790s and partly because of their impeccable character. However, at about the same time, the 'discoverers' of Piltdown man were also thought to be above suspicion.

The ladies' ghostly experience, if it can be believed, was not momentary like Toynbee's but lasted some hours. In England in 1793, a year or so after the events the ladies had envisioned, Wordsworth also had a strange vision of the past. He was much preoccupied by events across the Channel; his high hopes of the Revolution had been dashed and he was angry, anxious and perplexed by the bloody turn of events in France where he had left Annette Vallon to bear his child alone. As a result of an accident to the 'whiskey' in which he was touring with his friend Calvert, he spent three days alone walking on Salisbury plain 'the bare white roads lengthening in solitude their dreary line', and surrounded by the evidence of prehistoric times. Was it partly as a displacement for his present anxieties over the war (as with Henry James) that he spent those three days almost continuously in what he calls 'an antiquarian's dream'? For part of that time, and it is not clear for how long, it may only have been a moment, he had a vision which he calls 'an influx' and 'a privilege', 'Proceeding from the depth of untaught things'.

> While through those vestiges of ancient times
> I ranged, and by the solitude overcome,
> I had a reverie and saw the past,
> Saw multitudes of men, and here and there,
> A single Briton in his wolf-skin vest
> With shield and stone-axe, stride across the Wold;
> The voice of spears was heard, the rattling spear
> Shaken by arms of mighty bone, in strength
> Long moulder'd of barbaric majesty.
> I called upon the Darkness; and it took,
> A midnight darkness seem'd to come and take
> All objects from my sight; and lo! again
> The Desert visible by dismal flames!
> It is the sacrificial Altar, fed
> With living men, how deep the groans, the voice
> Of those in the gigantic wicker thrills
> Throughout the region far and near, pervades
> The monumental hillocks; and the pomp
> Is for both worlds, the living and the dead.

This passage comes in that part of *The Prelude* which is devoted to Wordsworth's account of the power of Imagination and is addressed to Coleridge. Like many of the Romantics, Wordsworth had been attracted by legends of Druids: Keats says,

There is a pleasure in the heath where Druids old have been,
Where mantles grey have rustled by and swept the nettled green.

and Wordsworth knew that pleasure. However, it is important to remember the extreme matter-of-factness and meticulous accuracy of Wordsworth's narrative in *The Prelude* and not to mistake his frightening vision for a piece of Gothick fancy. The strangest of Toynbee's experiences, quoted above, when he was 'directly aware of the passage of History gently flowing through him in a mighty current' has many similarities to other of Wordsworth's experiences. We may suppose the dawn view of London from Westminster Bridge recorded in a famous sonnet was one. An earlier example occurred at Christmas time in 1789 when, 'having thridded the long labyrinth of the suburban villages', he was entering London as a passenger on the top of the stage coach from Cambridge for the first time. Toynbee had been walking by Victoria Station, an 'incongruously prosaic' setting, as he says, for a mental illumination; Wordsworth, too, was surrounded not by 'natural objects' but by mean streets, and on realizing he had entered London . . .

> A weight of ages did at once descend
> Upon my heart; no thought embodied, no
> Distinct remembrances, but weight and power, –
> Power growing under weight: alas! I feel
> That I am trifling: 'twas a moment's pause, –
> All that took place within me came and went
> As in a moment; yet with Time it dwells,
> And grateful memory, as a thing divine.

This aweful experience of the weight of ages pressing down upon his heart left even Wordsworth at a loss for words. Like Toynbee's experience, it was momentary but momentous, it occurred entirely unexpectedly and in ordinarily uninspiring surroundings. Both experiences have similarities to those moments of 'impossible union' and 'belonging to the Universe' which were chronicled in chapter 4, and both, I suppose, might be seen as that common feeling for the romance of history which leads countless people to visit castles, abbeys, battlefields, great houses and museums but suddenly discharged with an *un*common degree of depth and intensity.

One further example here must suffice, and it is an interesting one in confirming the close links between the overwhelmingly sudden sense of the past and the pan-en-henic or nature-mystical experience. It comes from the autobiography of the novelist and critic, John Wain, who tells us that he had a lonely childhood and an instinctive reverence for nature which has never entirely left him.

For example: one day in the 1950's, a warm, soggy, sullen afternoon in autumn, I happened to be standing in the quadrangle of
an Oxford college. I was in the middle of a busy day, and my
thoughts were of work and sociability, of books, ideas, and people.
Suddenly, looking up, I saw a swan flying in a leisurely, deliberate
straight line right over my head, just above the level of the roof-
tops; in that marshy air, its broad, heavy wings flapping quite
slowly, it seemed almost to be swimming rather than flying. A few
strong, purposeful wingbeats and it was gone; but in an instant I
had realised, with a sharp physical intensity, the fact that all my
scurrying to and fro, talking, comparing ideas, gossiping, dis-
cussing personalities, was limited, contained, held in and at the
same time supported by the green earth, the grey stones, the
stretches of water and weed. I suddenly saw beyond the libraries,
the lectures, the talk, to what underlay them: the fact that men had
come to a meadowy river-bank under a grey and white sky, and
had decided on it as the site of a town, and reared these stone walls
and towers. And centuries later, here I stood, and the rushes still
grew on the banks, and the air still lay as heavily as water, and
above my head the great kingly bird flapped, from one stretch of
river to another, as it had done a thousand years ago – and we
were all, the bird and I and the men who had hewn the stones, and
the other men who had written the books on the library shelves,
and the earth-worms in the soil, the fish in the river, and the dogs
running about the streets, all living together in one eternity, here
and now on this earth: the eternity of nature.[6]

The experience swept him back beyond the man-made
environment, notwithstanding its venerable hewn stones, to
'the eternity of nature'. Apart from the astronomer's unimaginable light years, no facts are better calculated to 'wrench
out the roots of finitude' than those prodigious strata of time
before the beginning of human history whose only record is
in the unhewn stones. It is hardly surprising that geologists,
amateur and professional, of the last century, and, no doubt,
of later generations, encountered in their studies an awe that
was often absent from their religion and even read into the
record of the rocks fragments of a stoical ethic. Godwin Peak,
the hero of George Gissing's *Born in Exile* and, like others of
Gissing's heroes, bearing many resemblances to the author,
describes in a letter how he spent one Sunday (significantly a
Sunday) geologizing.

. . . a curious experience befel me . . . sitting down before some
interesting strata, I lost myself in something like nirvana, grew so

subject to the idea of vastness in geological time that all human desires and purposes shrivelled to ridiculous unimportance.

Immediately before, he had been tormented by the pangs of unrequited love but now, 'Awaking for a minute, I tried to realise the passion which not long ago rent and racked me' and lo! it was gone. Sermons in stones had done him more good than any from the pulpit would have done.

It may be, however, that a sudden revelation of the immensity of geological time is the beginning rather than the end of a passion, a passion for finding out. René Cutforth was an eleven-year-old at a Prep. school in Leicestershire whose official mental and physical regimen left him untouched except by boredom. The mathematics, the science and the history he was required to learn were 'mere lumps of unamenable fact, mere anxieties rolling in the void'. Cricket was as bad.

At this ungainly moment in my life it would have occurred to nobody, and least of all to me, that on the very next day I was to see a great light. It happened on a run. The weather was so bad at the beginning of that term that cricket was impossible, so after lunch, we all sloshed off in the rain in a straggling column across country, shepherded by Mr Johnson, an unhappy intellectual to whom these chores fell as by some natural law. After about a mile and a half I was leaning against a gate between two sodden lengths of cow pasture, getting my breath back, when I suddenly saw in the scuffed mud patch under the gate a piece of stone washed clear by the rain, and, contained in it, an intricate and perfect ribbed coil, like a coiled up snake, in a sort of dull gold. It was a beautiful object and a splendid find, and I was just wondering whether I could possibly carry it back, or should I hide it somewhere to be recovered on Sunday when I didn't have to run, when Mr Johnson appeared, more than inclined to lean on the same gate and get his breath back. 'Oh, sir,' I said, 'what's this?' 'That's an ammonite,' said Mr Johnson, puffing and blowing, 'a fossil shell, very old, used to live here when all this land was under the sea a long time ago.'
'Before the Romans and Ancient Britons?' I asked.
'Oh, long before, about sixty million years ago, before there were any men at all,' he said. 'At least, I think that's right, they seem to change the estimate about every five years.'
'Sixty million years old? Before or after the world was made in six days?'
'Well, metaphorically,' Mr Johnson said, 'about the Thursday of that week. An interesting period geologically: the giant lizards,

the dinosaurs, the first flying beasts, the pterodactyls – they're all here still under the ground. This part of England is full of them.'

I don't know why this revelation of the huge continuity of the past should have been such a release to my imagination, but it was. It was a genuine illumination – something to do with perspective, something to do with the mysterious quality of time itself. Something to do with buried treasure, something which joined the separate worlds of poetry and finding out and learning and digging and the splendid look of the country. Something which put cricket in its pettifogging place. During that summer I rarely emerged from the Jurassic Age. I found a quarry full of ammonites and belemnites and terebratulae and rhynconellae and gryphaea and pecten and sea urchins. A whole sea bottom of creatures who'd lived and died and left themselves to be explained – this was the point – before anybody could have possibly explained them. With great difficulty I read that holy book, *The Origin of Species*. I sent for everything the South Kensington Museum had published about the Jurassic and the Lower Lias. I knew the names of all the creatures.[7]

In the same way that the words 'Siegfried and the Twilight of the Gods' led C. S. Lewis to devour anything and everything he could lay his hands on connected with the Wagnerian mythology, so that ammonite from the Lower Lias awoke René Cutforth intellectually at about the same age. Whether intentionally or by accident, the weedy Mr Johnson had held the murmuring shell of time to his ear and kindled a spark of romance, a sense of wonder. When he stopped by the gate in the rain and talked to the small boy instead of telling him to 'cut along' – a phrase with the right period flavour – he was *teaching* and anything less important than that is only called 'teaching' by courtesy.

Just as the moment of the rose is a superlative brief moment of glory, a tremor of bliss which goes beyond any meaning we can assign to happiness, so the moment of the yew tree is an inexplicable visionary dreariness darkening at times into abject desolation and terror. It is a 'dysphoric' rather than a euphoric experience, often a prolonged struggle in the slough of despond, more rarely a sudden terrifying slip down a seemingly bottomless precipice. That very sense of the past which we have been exploring in the last chapter may precipitate a desolation experience: 'Thousands of human generations,' says Carlyle, 'all as noisy as our own, have been swallowed up of Time, and there remains no wreck of them any more.' Like Tennyson's mild-eyed melancholy Lotos Eaters, it may make us feel the utter futility of any human endeavour:

> Time driveth onward fast,
> And in a little while our lips are dumb.
> Let us alone. What is it that will last?
> All things are taken from us and become
> Portions and parcels of the dreadful Past.

The Lotos Eaters may have imagined they could spend an eternity 'careless of mankind' and 'propt on beds of amaranth and moly', but in reality it is often only one short step from the rose garden into the shadow of the yew. 'The melancholy fit fell very suddenly,' notes Barbellion in his Journal for 11 June 1913, when the roses were at their best. 'All the colour went out of my life, the world was dirty grey.'

In chapter 5 we have already quoted C. Day Lewis's account of a sunlit summer moment of love and joy which was preceded by a 'grey drizzle'. He says in the same place:

About this time – my eighteenth or nineteenth year – began those periodical black moods, unfocussed, unintelligible, irresistible, which for many years were to sweep over me out of the blue, drenching me with misery and rendering me so morally impotent that I could not descry any gleam of reassurance through their mirk, nor make the least move to free myself. I learnt later that theologians knew it as a deadly sin, accidie. But I also learnt by experience that these moods were often fore-runners of a new burst of poetic activity, as though I must go down into the utter darkness before the seeds of light in me could germinate.[1]

Chaucer called accidie this 'roten herted sinne'. We do not know whether he was troubled by it but in his day it was supposed to be particularly prevalent in the cheerless months after Christmas. They were often hungry months, too, and very likely the effect of lack of light and a lean diet on the chemistry of the body may have had something to do with it. It was regarded spiritually as an occupational hazard of monks and hermits and attracted much attention from the desert fathers of the fourth century. Many poets down the ages, besides Chaucer, have experienced accidie – whatever they called it – though they would mostly have regarded it as an *affliction*, for it would be hard indeed if anything so irresistible should be a *sin*. The Romantic poets were notable in giving it a voice.

> How languidly I look
> Upon the visible fabric of this world.

groans Wordsworth in Book III of *The Excursion* which he called 'Despondency'. He knew that it was the power of the mind with its internal weather that transformed the perceived world from Paradise into a joyless desert when all seems vanity and vexation of spirit.

Coleridge likewise, when he genial spirits failed, gazed on the moonlit night 'with how blank an eye' and experienced

> A grief without a pang, void, dark and drear.
> A stifled, drowsy, unimpassioned grief,
> Which finds no natural outlet, no relief . . .

In his famous *Ode*, it is precisely the absence of those moments of joy and inspiration out of which poetry is born which characterize his dejection. Under the darkness of the yew, he felt, nothing germinated, nothing grew.

Keats, too, who had more real cause for dejection than either Wordsworth or Coleridge in the year of his great odes, 1819, is like them in realizing that it is the man who 'Can burst

Joy's grape against the palate' who must also pay the penalty of that 'wakeful anguish of the soul'. By feeding it on beauty, however, he thought melancholy could be transformed into something luxuriant rather than arid. Leigh Hunt, a friend of all the others, is but one more. Reflecting on his youth he exclaims, 'What pangs of biliary will and impossibility I underwent in the endeavour to solve those riddles of the universe – I felt, long before I knew Mr Wordsworth's poetry

> the burden of the mystery
> Of all this unintelligible world.

And Wordsworth's poety was to help John Stuart Mill to grope his way out of a similar baffled despondency.

No doubt melancholy has more shades of grey than even the indefatigable Burton could anatomize but in so far as it is 'a grief without a pang' it is a state contrasted to cheerfulness or contentment rather than a 'nadir' experience. In Carlyle's terms we might call it the 'Centre of Indifference' but biased towards the Everlasting No rather than the Everlasting Yea. That it can be concentrated into a timeless moment, memorable with a shudder of awe for a lifetime, we must now show from some more modern instances.

Leonard Woolf was no more than five years old when he had what he calls 'My first experience of Weltschmerz . . . a wave of that profound cosmic melancholia which is hidden in every human heart.'

I can remember returning one late, chilly September afternoon to Lexham Gardens from our holiday and rushing out eagerly to see the back garden. There it lay in its grimy solitude. There was not a breath of air. There were no flowers; a few spindly lilac bushes drooped in the beds. The grimy ivy drooped on the grimy walls. And over all the walls from ivy leaf to ivy leaf were large or small spiderwebs, dozens and dozens of them, quite motionless, and motionless in the centre of each web sat a large or a small, a fat or a lean spider. I stood by myself in the patch of scurfy grass and contemplated the spiders; I can still smell the smell of sour earth and ivy; and suddenly my whole mind and body seemed to be overwhelmed in melancholy. I did not cry, though there were, I think, tears in my eyes; I had experienced cosmic unhappiness which comes upon us when those that look out of windows be darkened, when the daughters of music are laid low, the doors are shut in the street, the sound of the grinding is low, the grasshopper is a burden and desire fails.

Certainly the Old Testament prophets and poets knew the 'aridity' of wandering in the spiritual desert which the mediaeval mystics also called 'the dark night of the soul': we can only suppose that they also knew this black flash of lightning. Three years later, when he was eight years old, Leonard Woolf was absorbed in watching some newts when he had another experience in which, quite literally, 'The black cloud carries the sun away' and he was struck by another black flash.

> I do not know how long I had sat there when, all at once, I felt afraid. I looked up and saw that an enormous black thunder cloud had just crept up and now covered more than half of the sky. It was just blotting out the sun, and, as it did so, the newts scuttled back into their hole. It was terrifying and, no doubt, I was terrified. But I felt something more powerful than fear, once more that sense of profound, passive, cosmic despair, the melancholy of a human being, eager for happiness and beauty, powerless in the face of a hostile universe. As the great raindrops began to fall and the thunder to mutter and growl over the sea, I crept back into the house with a curious muddle of fear, contempt, scepticism, and fatalism in my childish mind.[2]

Virginia Woolf, who knew at first hand, too, with terrifying intensity, the moment of the yew tree, described through the mouth of one of her characters in *The Waves* those moments of 'cosmic despair' as 'this devastating sense of grey ashes in a burnt-out grate'. Her husband has himself drawn attention to the similarity between what he experienced and an autobiographical fragment in one of Thomas Traherne's Meditations.

> Another time in a lowering and sad evening, being alone in the field, when all things were dead and quiet, a certain want and horror fell upon me, beyond imagination. The unprofitableness and silence of the place dissatisfied me; its wideness terrified me; from the utmost ends of the earth fears surrounded me. How did I know but dangers might suddenly arise from the East and invade me from unknown regions beyond the seas? I was a weak and little child, and had forgotten there was a man alive in the earth.[3]

Wordsworth was also only five years old, in 'the twilight of rememberable life' when he, too, had his first experience of Weltschmerz or 'visionary dreariness' as he calls it. He sometimes accidentally ante-dates events but this one must certainly have belonged to quite early boyhood, before he was sent to board at Hawkshead school at the age of nine. He was staying at his mother's old home at Penrith and went out riding with James, the groom, on the east side of Penrith Beacon. Having become accidentally separated from his companion, he wandered lost on the desolate moor until he chanced on a mouldered gibbet with the murderer's name still visible cut in the turf. 'Faltering and faint, and ignorant of the road' he fled to where he could see a naked pool and a girl with a pitcher on her head struggling against the wind.[4]

It is not surprising that it was a frightening experience to a five-year-old, but it was not just the fear that he remembered: the experience was in his view valuable and worth recording because the fear etched on his mind with lasting vividness the whole desolate scene with its naked pool and beacon and wind-blown girl.

Wordsworth had grown up 'fostered alike by beauty and by fear' and it is the joys *and fears* of the human heart for which he gives thanks at the end of the 'Immortality' ode. In chapter 3 we suggested that strong emotions seem to be responsible for sometimes fixing in the memory indelibly quite ordinary scenes or objects. This was certainly Wordsworth's experience. A murderer's epitaph is not, perhaps, an everyday sight, nor is a dead bather rising bolt upright with his ghastly face from the surface of beautiful Esthwaite Water; these two incidents belong to early childhood. A commoner and less 'gothick' fear was associated with the danger of physical exploits like skating at night or bird-nesting, when the young Wordsworth

hung
Above the raven's nest, by knots of grass
And half-inch fissures in the slippery rock.

Then the voice of the loud dry wind and the movement of the clouds would remain with him always.

Dr Johnson held, as everybody knows, that the prospect of hanging concentrates a man's mind wonderfully and it is certainly the case that imminent danger can stimulate awareness and cleanse the doors of perception. Camus' outsider-hero Mersault begins consciously to appreciate the ordinary sights and sounds of existence to which he had previously been indifferent as the date of his execution grows nearer, and

Baron Toozenbach, in Chekhov's *The Three Sisters*, before his duel says:

> I feel quite elated. I feel as if I was seeing these fir-trees and maples and birches for the first time in my life. They all seem to be looking at me with a sort of inquisitive look and waiting for something.

Guilt is a species of fear which seems to have been a particularly potent emotion for Wordsworth: the occasion when he stole a skiff for a moonlight row on Ullswater and the woodcock-snaring incident when he took 'the captive of another's toil' are among the most vivid recorded in the first book of *The Prelude*.

But experiences of 'visionary dreariness' or 'want and horror beyond imagination' are by no means always confined to childhood. C. Day Lewis was about eighteen before such experiences began and Hugh Fausset was the same age when, on a single evening, he plunged from the heights to the abyss. In chapter 9 we quoted his beatific experience of identity with the creative will on a fell top near his father's rectory in northern England. 'How transitory,' he says, 'was my assurance that all was ultimately well with life was revealed by the experience of the demonic which succeeded my intuition of the divine.'

> It was between ten and eleven at night before I began to descend, and compared to the luminosity of the heights, the lower levels were sunk in darkness. The further I proceeded, stumbling through heather or surprising a resting sheep into ungainly flight, the more depressed my spirits became. And it was not a merely negative depression. A sense of impalpable malignity, combined with a strange terror, grew upon me until I felt even the hills behind, above and around me to be closing in, united in a conspiracy to crush all that was individual in me and to pile themselves like some vast cromlech, over the corpse of my human identity.[5]

Such archetypal experiences have led to the picture, common to many cultures, of man's pilgrimage as a middle way through a cosmic struggle between light and dark, Good and Evil, yang and yin. At the age of seventeen, Colin Wilson had what was, physically speaking, an ordinary brief black-out, but mentally a glimpse of the heart of darkness which may not have been insignificant in forming his philosophy. Out of boredom, he had spent the whole day reading:

I went into the kitchen to switch on the stove to make tea, and had a blackout. It was a strange sensation. I stood there fully conscious, clutching the stove to keep upright, and yet conscious of nothing but blackness. There was an electric-like sensation in my brain, so that I could readily have believed that I had been given an electric shock. It was as if something were flowing through me, and I had an insight of what lay on the other side of consciousness. It looked like an eternity of pain. When my vision cleared, I switched on the kettle and went into the other room. I could not be certain what I had seen, but I was afraid of it. It seemed as if I were the bed of a river, and the current was all pain. I thought I had seen the final truth *that life does not lead to anything*; it is an *escape from something*, and the 'something' is a horror that lies on the other side of consciousness. I could understand what Kurtz had seen in Heart of Darkness. All the metaphysical doubts of years seemed to gather to a point, in one realisation: what *use* is such a truth?[6]

Two lines in Wordsworth's early tragedy, *The Borderers*, suggest that he, too, knew some such frightful vision of an 'eternity of pain'.

> Suffering is permanent, obscure and dark
> And shares the nature of infinity.

Colin Wilson asks what use is such an insight. Wordsworth would have said it can be made to humanize the soul and help us to be more acutely conscious of 'the still, sad music of humanity'. If man is to endure such a vision he must find a light to lighten the darkness; the yang and yin must inter-inanimate fruitfully. Bertrand Russell provides an interesting example of how a desolation experience of this type may, in certain circumstances, rebound into life-changing, euphoric altruism.

Mrs Whitehead was at this time becoming more and more of an invalid, and used to have intense pain owing to heart trouble. She seemed cut off from everyone and everything by walls of agony, and the sense of the solitude of each human soul suddenly overwhelmed me.

Ever since my marriage, my emotional life had been calm and superficial. I had forgotten all the deeper issues, and had been content with flippant cleverness. Suddenly the ground seemed to give way beneath me, and I found myself in quite another region. Within five minutes I went through some such reflections as the following: the loneliness of the human soul is unendurable; nothing can penetrate it except the highest intensity of the sort of love that religious teachers have preached; whatever does not spring from this motive is harmful, or at best useless; it follows that war is wrong, that a public school education is abominable, that the use of force is to be deprecated, and that in human relations one should penetrate to the core of loneliness in each person and speak to that . . .

At the end of those five minutes, I had become a completely different person. For a time, a sort of mystic illumination possessed me. I felt that I knew the inmost thoughts of everybody that I met in the street, and though this was, no doubt, a delusion, I did in actual fact find myself in far closer touch than previously with all my friends, and many of my acquaintances. Having been an Imperialist, I became during those five minutes a pro-Boer and a Pacifist. Having for years cared only for exactness and analysis, I now found myself filled with semi-mystical feelings about beauty, with an intense interest in children . . .

The mystic insight which I then imagined myself to possess has largely faded, and the habit of analysis has reasserted itself. But something of what I thought I saw in that moment has remained always with me, causing my attitude during the first war, my interest in children, my indifference to minor misfortunes, and a certain emotional tone in all my human relations.[7]

'That moment has remained,' says Russell. The moment of the yew tree is timeless, like the moment of the rose: 'moments of agony' as Eliot puts it, 'are likewise permanent'.

> We appreciate this better
> In the agony of others, nearly experienced,
> Involving ourselves, than in our own.
> For our own past is covered by the currents of action,
> But the torment of others remains an experience
> Unqualified, unworn by subsequent attrition.[8]

Our own agony, too, can cut us off from others. When the black mood came, Coleridge said

> . . . each visitation
> Suspends what nature gave me at my birth,
> My shaping spirit of Imagination.

It was not just that it cut him off from poetic inspiration, for the imagination, as Coleridge is never tired of preaching, enables us to put ourselves in the place of others, to feel what they are feeling and thence to sympathize and love. Little wonder that C. Day Lewis in his black moods of drenching misery described himself as being '*morally* impotent'.

We have already, in the last chapter, stolen 'the backward

look behind the assurance of recorded history'. It remains here to document 'the backward half-look over the shoulder, towards the primitive terror'. All kinds of nameless dread inhabit the yew tree's shade. Canon Raven, from whom we have already quoted in chapter 5, was a 'bug-hunter' in his teens, a pursuit which led him into such nocturnal shades.

> A wood may speak life: the fens speak only of eternity. Standing alone in their immensity you are in the presence chamber of the infinite, and an ancient awe whispers panic and makes trial of the fibre of your manhood. You are stripped stark: excuses, vanities, sophistries are unavailing; only the elemental simplicities remain. No one can know what nature can mean until he has spent such a vigil alone in the night.[9]

From the fens of East Anglia to the hills of Wicklow and we find J. M. Synge encountering the same grisly aspect of the *mysterium tremendum* and being 'menaced by monsters' in his pursuit of lepidoptera.

> Natural history did much for me. To wander as I did for years through the dawn of night with every nerve stiff and strained with expectation gives one a singular acquaintance with the essences of the world. The obscure noises of the owls and rabbits, the heavy scent of the hemlock and the flowers of the elder, and the silent flight of the moths I was in search of gave me a passionate and receptive mood like that of early man . . .
> One evening when I was collecting moths on the brow of a long valley in County Wicklow curious wreaths of white mist began to rise from the narrow bogs near the river. A little before dark I looked round the edge of the field and saw two immense luminous eyes staring at me from the base of the valley. I dropped my net and caught hold of the gate in front of me. Behind the eyes there rose a black sinister forehead. I was horrified. For a moment the eyes seemed to consume my personality, then the whole valley became filled with a pageant of movement and colour, and the opposite hillside covered itself with ancient doorways and spires and high turrets. I did not know where or when I was existing. Suddenly someone spoke in the lane behind me – it was a labourer going home – and I came back to myself.[10]

Though this experience had a simple natural explanation, the author goes on to say, 'For many days I could not look on those fields even in daylight without shuddering.'

The terror that overwhelmed Hugh Fausset threatened, as he says 'to crush . . . my human identity' and Synge's apparition 'seemed to consume my personality'. Similarly with John Addington Symonds: he had a disturbing kind of trance which recurred over many years with diminishing frequency until he was twenty-eight and was the opposite of a pleasurable rapture and self-absorption which he also knew. It might come when he was alone or in company but always when his muscles were relaxed, he says, and, after lasting what seemed an eternity, diminish like the effect of an anaesthetic.

> I cannot even now find words to render it intelligible, although it is probable that many readers of these pages will recognise the state in question. It consisted in a gradual but swiftly progressive obliteration of space, time, sensation, and the multitudinous factors of experience which seem to qualify what we are pleased to call ourself. In proportion, as these conditions of ordinary consciousness were subtracted, the sense of an underlying or essential consciousness acquired intensity. At last nothing remained but a pure, absolute, abstract self. The universe became without form and void of content. But self persisted, formidable in its vivid keenness, feeling the most poignant doubt about reality, ready, as it seemed, to find existence break as breaks a bubble round about it. And what then? The apprehension of a coming dissolution, the grim conviction that this state was the last state of the conscious self . . .[11]

Just as the moment of the rose is often ecstatic in the strict sense of making us 'beside ourselves', so the moment of the yew tree is an internal darkness which threatens to extinguish the self in its depth. Each is a kind of madness. 'I tremble to think', says Mark Rutherford, 'how thin is the floor on which we stand, which separates us from the bottomless abyss.' Throughout his life he was plagued by fits of deepest depression which he called 'the enemy' and 'the horrible Python'. His second son wrote that 'No account of my father would be trustworthy which did not duly bring out the disconsolate moods which were frequent with him.' The following is an account of one such occasion. In 1852 at the age of twenty-one and shortly after his expulsion from theological college for holding unorthodox views, he arrived as a teacher at a Unitarian School at Stoke Newington a few days before term began. He was given supper in an empty school-room and then went up to his bedroom.

I ascended and found a little chamber, dull, furnished with a chest of drawers, bed, and washhand-stand. It was tolerably clean and decent; but who shall describe what I felt? I went to the window and looked out. There were scattered lights here and there, marking roads, but as they crossed one another, and now and then stopped where building had ceased, the effect they produced was that of bewilderment with no clue to it. Further off was the great light of London, like some unnatural dawn, or the illumination from a fire which could not itself be seen. I was overcome with the most dreadful sense of loneliness. I suppose it is the very essence of passion, using the word in its literal sense, that no account of it can be given by the reason . . . I was beside myself with a kind of terror, which I cannot further explain. It is possible for another person to understand grief for the death of a friend, bodily suffering, or any emotion which has a distinct cause, but how shall he under-stand the worst of all calamities, the nameless dread, the efflux of all vitality, the ghostly, haunting horror which is so nearly akin to madness?[12]

There is some evidence for suggesting that people who plumb these depths are also likely to scale the heights. It has often been suggested that highly creative people in general, scientists as well as artists, may experience both the moment of the rose and of the yew tree more commonly than others or, to put it in medical parlance, that they often show some symptoms of the manic depressive psychosis. The manic state of near-frenzy or prolonged euphoria in which *some* artists in history have produced their best work so that they seemed both to them-selves and others to be possessed has been recognized as bordering on insanity since the earliest times: according to Seneca, Aristotle held that 'Nullum magnum ingenium sine mixtura dementiae fuit.' Similarly, depression has sometimes been seen as the darkness in which either the seeds of artistic creation begin to germinate, as Day Lewis suggested, or that dark night of the soul before the most radiant faith dawns.

Tolstoy in the middle way, approaching fifty, was plunged into such a darkness. Whereas other writers we have quoted feared the experience would destroy them, he was afraid it would make him destroy himself.

I felt that something had broken within me on which my life had always rested, and that I had nothing left to hold on to, that morally my life had stopped. An invincible force impelled me to get rid of my existence, in one way or another. It cannot be said that I wished to kill myself, for the force that drew me away from life was fuller, more powerful, more general than any mere desire. It was a force like my old aspiration to live – only it impelled me in the opposite direction. It was an aspiration of my whole being to get out of life.

Behold me then a happy man in good health, hiding the rope in order not to hang myself to the rafters of my room where every night I went to sleep alone; behold me no longer going shooting, lest I yield to the too easy temptation of putting an end to myself with my gun.

I did not know what I wanted. I was afraid of life; I was driven to leave it; and in spite of that I still hoped for something from it.

All this took place at a time when so far as all my outward circumstances went I ought to have been completely happy. I had a good wife who loved me and whom I loved, good children and a large property which was increasing with no pains taken on my part . . .

I was like one lost in a wood who, horrified at having lost his way, rushes about wishing to find the road. He knows that each step he takes confuses him more and more, but still he cannot help rushing about.

It was indeed terrible. And to rid myself of the terror I wished to kill myself . . .

I sought in all the sciences, but far from finding what I wanted, became convinced that all who like myself had sought in knowledge for the meaning of life had found nothing. And not only had they found nothing, but they had plainly acknowledged that the very thing that made me despair – namely the senselessness of life – is the one indubitable thing man can know.[13]

Tolstoy was lost in this dark wood, bramble and grimpen for *two years* of agony. Today, no doubt, he would have been treated with anti-depressant drugs or electro-convulsive therapy and returned to the world as cured in a few weeks. This raises some very interesting questions, for the story of his terrible ordeal is only the beginning of his Confession: it is only the darkness in which was forged the faith and philosophy which sustained his vigorous later years. Just as genius and madness are near allied and often hard to tell apart, so we must doubt whether we are competent to distinguish between religion and insanity. Should George Fox, running up and down the streets deluded that they were rivers of blood and crying 'Woe to the bloody city of Lichfield', have been certified insane and treated accordingly? M. O'C. Drury has recently suggested that if Robert de Baudricourt could have given Joan of

Arc a stiff dose of phenothiazine no more would have been heard of the voices of St Michael and St Catherine telling her to drive the English out of France. At a more commonplace level, loss of faith and other spiritual crises are often, to the psychiatrist, straightforward cases of depression or involutional melancholia and will yield remarkably rapidly to modern drugs. It would be hard to tell a doctor that he should not relieve acute mental suffering because, once in a while, he might be depriving the world of a saint or the last sonnets of a Gerard Manley Hopkins. It is the sort of choice Aldous Huxley was predicting over forty years ago that we should have to make in our brave new world.

The paradoxical world in which

Our only health is the disease

is not the world in which most of us would choose to live our everyday lives; but all through our lives in that everyday world there come moments of intersection with another dimension which can only be spoken of in a language that *is* paradoxical and logically odd.

The last thing we need to say about the moment of the rose and the moment of the yew tree is that they are not far apart, not at opposite extremes like the peaks and troughs of a fever chart. In that other dimension it is as if the flat two-dimensional graph was taken and rolled horizontally into a cylinder until the peaks and troughs touched, the way up and the way down led to the same place and the paradoxes were reconciled.

Since this has been a book of quotations, others must have the last words, and not the great mystics but people who were ordinary except, perhaps, in being more than ordinarily creative, articulate and attentive to their unattended moments.

On the South American pampas, Hudson, like so many other children, had glimpsed a place where the rose and the yew grew side by side.

The sight of a magnificent sunset was sometimes more than I could endure and made me wish to hide myself away. The feeling was, however, evoked more powerfully by trees than by any other sight; it varied in power according to the time and place and the appearance of the tree or trees, and always affected me most on moonlight nights. Frequently, after I had first begun to experience it consciously, I would go out of my way to meet it, and I used to steal out of the house alone when the moon was at its full to stand, silent and motionless, near some group of large trees, gazing at the dusky green foliage silvered by the beams; and at such times the sense of mystery would grow until a sensation of delight would change to fear, and the fear increase until it was no longer to be borne, and I would hastily escape to recover the sense of reality and safety indoors, where there was light and company.[14]

From joy through awe to a shuddering dread the wheel turns one way. It may equally well swing the other way from desolation to joy, from under the yew tree into the sunlit rose garden with the sound of children 'hidden excitedly, containing laughter', from the shadow of mortality to an intimation of eternal life. Sybil Thorndike went down to Rainham in Kent early in the Second World War and wrote later to a friend about what happened there.

I was packing up a house for my son – he had gone off to sea, and his wife and family had gone off to our house in Wales. The furniture van had left, the house was empty and I, feeling a little forlorn, was wandering round the garden thinking of the happy jolly times we'd had while they were living there. I caught sight, in a flower bed, of a bright-coloured ball, which suddenly made me cry, and all at once I seemed to be in a changed atmosphere. It was a little alarming at first. Everything looked the same but seemed charged with something more real – very hard to explain. It was as if suddenly, for a flash, I was seeing the significance of things – material things being just symbols – like seeing familiar things on another plane of existence. This curious feeling lasted about ten minutes, and then I was back to normal – but in those few moments I had sensed great happiness and a sureness of something that I felt was eternal life.[15]

And so, 'the end of all our exploring Will be to arrive where we started' – at the moment of the rose. Macbeth's astonished exclamation might be a fitting post-script not to this experience only but to all those we have quoted in this book.

> Can such things be
> And overcome us like a summer's cloud
> Without our special wonder?

Notes and Sources

The quotation opposite the title page from T. S. Eliot, *The Dry Salvages*, is used by kind permission of Faber & Faber.

Introduction

1. Weidenfeld & Nicolson 1963.
2. Walter Pater, 'The Child in the House', *Miscellaneous Studies*, Macmillan, NY 1907, p. 158. First published in *Macmillan's Magazine*, August 1878.
3. Julian Huxley, *Religion without Revelation*, Max Parrish 1957, p. 70. Reprinted by permission of A. D. Peters & Co. Ltd.
4. C. E. Montague, *A Writer's Notes on his Trade*, Chatto & Windus 1930. Used by permission of the publisher and Mrs Rose Elton.

Chapter 1

1. Willa Muir, *Belonging: a memoir*, The Hogarth Press 1968, p. 14. Used by permission of the publisher and Mr Gavin Muir.
2. Elizabeth Hamilton, *An Irish Childhood*, Chatto & Windus 1963, pp. 26–7.
3. Mary Austin, *Experiences Facing Death*, Rider & Co. 1931, pp. 24–5.
4. Vicars Bell, *Steep Ways and Narrow*, Faber & Faber 1963, pp. 22–3.
5. Richard Jefferies, *The Story of My Heart*, 1883; Constable 1947, pp. 58–9.
6. Margiad Evans, *A Ray of Darkness*, Arthur Barker 1952, pp. 163–4.
7. L. E. Jones, *A Victorian Boyhood*, Macmillan 1955, pp. 168–9.
8. Forrest Reid, *Apostate*, Constable 1926, p. 149; Faber & Faber 1947. Reprinted by permission of Faber & Faber.
9. Richard Hillyer, *Country Boy*, Hodder & Stoughton 1966, p. 101. Used by permission of the author.
10. Julian Huxley, *Religion without Revelation*, p. 79.
11. Morag Coate, *Beyond All Reason*, Constable 1964, p. 21.

Chapter 2

1. Sir Kenneth Clark, *Moments of Vision* (Romanes Lecture 1954). Used by permission of the Oxford University Press, Oxford.
2. Llewelyn Powys, *Skin for Skin*, Jonathan Cape 1926, pp. 37–8. Used by permission of The Society of Authors as the literary representative of the Estate of Llewelyn Powys.
3. A. F. Webling, *Something Beyond: a life story*, CUP 1931, pp. 2–3.
4. Andrew Young, *The New Poly-Olbion*, Rupert Hart-Davis 1967, p. 26. Reprinted by permission of the author's literary executor, Mr Leonard Clark.
5. Vladimir Nabokov, *Speak, Memory*, Victor Gollancz 1951, pp. 155–6.
6. A. L. Rowse, *A Cornish Childhood*, Jonathan Cape 1954, pp. 215–16.
7. Sir Arthur Quiller-Couch, *Memories and Opinions*, CUP 1944, p. 52.

Chapter 3

1. William James, *The Principles of Psychology*, Macmillan 1902, vol. 1, ch. xvi, p. 643.
2. Longmans 1970.
3. T. F. Powys, *Soliloquies of a Hermit*, Andrew Melrose 1918, pp. 60–1.
4. Margiad Evans, *Autobiography*, Basil Blackwell 1943, p. 78.
5. Ibid., p. 94.
6. Basil Willey, *Spots of Time: a retrospect of the years 1897–1920*, Chatto & Windus 1965, pp. 94–5.
7. A. L. Rowse, *A Cornish Childhood*, pp. 85, 154.
8. Margaret Isherwood, *Searching for Meaning*, Allen & Unwin 1970, pp. 18–19.

Chapter 4

1. William James, *The Varieties of Religious Experience*, Longmans 1902; Fontana 1960, p. 366.
2. Osbert Sitwell, *Left Hand, Right Hand*, Macmillan 1945, pp. 178–9.
3. Willa Muir, *Belonging*, p. 14.
4. Forrest Reid, *Apostate*, p. 158.
5. Margiad Evans, *Autobiography*, p. 95.
6. Vladimir Nabokov, *Speak, Memory*, pp. 96–7.
7. Edward Carpenter, *Towards Democracy*, Allen & Unwin 1921, p. 515.
8. John Cowper Powys, *Autobiography*, The Bodley Head 1934, pp. 166–9; Macdonald & Co. 1967. Used by permission of the Estate of the late John Cowper Powys.
9. Faber & Faber 1931.
10. Sir Kenneth Clark, *Moments of Vision*. Used by permission of the Oxford University Press, Oxford.
11. Martin Buber, *Between Man and Man*, Routledge 1947; Fontana 1961, pp. 30–31, 43.
12. *Poetical Works of William Wordsworth*, ed. William Knight, 1896, vol. viii, p. 201.
13. Julian Huxley, *Memories*, Allen & Unwin 1970, pp. 53–5.
14. Richard Hillyer, *Country Boy*, pp. 140–1.
15. Jacquetta Hawkes, *Man on Earth*, Cresset Press 1954, pp. 15–17. Reprinted by permission of A. D. Peters & Co. Ltd.

Chapter 5

1. *The Dry Salvages* II in *Four Quartets*, Faber & Faber 1944.
2. Jacquetta Hawkes, *Man on Earth*, p. 16.
3. C. Day Lewis, *The Buried Day*, Chatto & Windus 1960, p. 120. Used by permission of the publisher and the author's Literary Estate.
4. Margaret Prescott Montague, *Twenty Minutes of Reality*, pp. 6ff., 25. Copyright 1917 by E. P. Dutton & Co. Inc., NY, and used by permission.
5. W. B. Yeats, *Per Amica Silentia Lunae*, Macmillan 1918, pp. 85f.
6. W. B. Yeats, Vacillation IV from 'The Winding Stair,' from *The Collected Poems of W. B. Yeats*. Both extracts used by permission of M. B. Yeats, Miss Anne Yeats and the Macmillan Company.
7. Hugh L'Anson Fausset, *A Modern Prelude*, Jonathan Cape 1933, pp. 169f. Used by permission of the publisher and the Executors of the Hugh L'Anson Fausset Estate.
8. Charles E. Raven, *A Wanderer's Way*, Martin Hopkinson 1929, pp. 83ff.

9. Leslie D. Weatherhead, *The Christian Agnostic*, Hodder & Stoughton 1965, pp. 39f.

10. Anthony Blond 1967.

11. Ida Gandy, *A Wiltshire Childhood*, Allen & Unwin 1929, pp. 160f., 140.

Chapter 6

1. Jean-Jacques Rousseau, from the fifth of the *Reveries*.

2. In a letter to Mr B. P. Blood. Quoted in *Memoirs of Alfred Tennyson*, ii, 473.

3. *John Addington Symonds*. A Biography compiled from his Papers and Correspondence by Horatio F. Brown, Smith, Elder & Co. 1903, p. 19.

4. Frank Conroy, *Stop Time*, The Bodley Head 1968, p. 104.

5. Edmund Gosse, *Father & Son*, 1907; Penguin 1947, pp. 230–1.

6. Forrest Reid, *Apostate*, p. 113.

7. Forrest Reid, *Private Road*, Faber & Faber 1940, pp. 124–5.

8. A. E. (George Russell), *The Candle of Vision*, Macmillan 1918, p. 2.

9. Thomas De Quincy, *Autobiography*, ed. Edward Sackville West, Cresset Press 1950, pp. 25–6.

Chapter 7

1. Richard Church, *Over the Bridge*, Heinemann 1955, pp. 167–8.

2. Arthur Koestler, *Arrow in the Blue*, Collins 1952, p. 51. Reprinted by permission of A. D. Peters & Co. Ltd.

3. Mary Antin, *The Promised Land*, Heinemann 1912, pp. 86–7. Reprinted by permission of Houghton Mifflin Company, Boston.

4. Mary Austin, *Earth Horizon*, Houghton Mifflin Company, Boston 1932, pp. 153–4.

5. Richard Maurice Bucke, *Cosmic Consciousness*, pp. 9–10. Copyright 1923 by E. P. A. Connaughton. Reprinted by permission of the publishers, E. P. Dutton & Co. Inc, NY.

6. William Soutar, 'Reality', *Collected Poems*, Andrew Dakers 1948, p. 276.

7. Arthur Koestler, *The Invisible Writing*, Collins and Hamish Hamilton 1954, pp. 350–3. Reprinted by permission of A. D. Peters & Co. Ltd.

Chapter 8

1. C. S. Lewis, *Surprised by Joy*, Geoffrey Bles 1955; Fontana 1959, pp. 18ff. Used by permission of Collins Publishers.

2. Yvonne Lubbock, *Return to Belief*, Collins 1961, p. 21.

3. A. E. Coppard, *It's Me, O Lord*, Methuen 1957, p. 206. Reprinted by permission of A. D. Peters & Co. Ltd.

4. *The Autobiography of J. M. Synge*, constructed from the Mss by Alan Price, OUP 1965, pp. 24–5.

5. W. N. P. Barbellion (Bruce Frederick Cummings), *The Journal of a Disappointed Man*, Chatto & Windus 1919, p. 90.

6. John Ruskin, *Modern Painters*, 1843ff., vol. 3.

Chapter 9

1. George Eliot, *The Mill on the Floss*, 1860, Book 2, ch. 1.

2. Forrest Reid, *Apostate*, pp. 198–9.

3. *The Prelude* (1805), Book XI, lines 258–68.

4. Morag Coate, *Beyond All Reason*, p. 14.

5. Rabindranath Tagore, *The Religion of Man*, Allen & Unwin, 3rd ed. 1949, pp. 94–6.

6. Virginia Woolf, *Mrs Dalloway*, The Hogarth Press 1947. Used by permission of the publisher and the author's Literary Estate.

7. Hugh L'Anson Fausset, *A Modern Prelude*, pp. 144ff.

Chapter 10

1. Cyril Connolly, *Enemies of Promise*, Routledge 1938, p. 215; André Deutsch 1973.

2. C. S. Lewis, *Surprised by Joy*, p. 62.

3. Gavin Maxwell, *The House of Elrig*, Longmans 1965, pp. 58–9. © Gavin Maxwell 1965. Reprinted by permission of Penguin Books Ltd.

4. Richard Church, *Over the Bridge*, pp. 224–5.

5. Mark Rutherford (William Hale White), *The Autobiography of Mark Rutherford*, 1881; OUP 1936, pp. 22–3.

6. A. F. Webling, *Something Beyond*, p. 67.

7. Warner Allen, *The Timeless Moment*, Faber & Faber 1946, p. 33. Reprinted by permission of the Estate of Warner Allen.

8. Basil Willey, *Spots of Time*, pp. 64–8.

Chapter 11

1. Edward Gibbon, *Autobiography*, J. M. Dent 1932, pp. 122–4.

2. Richard Jefferies, *The Story of My Heart*, pp. 36–7.

3. C. V. Wedgwood, *Truth and Opinion*, Collins 1969, p. 21.

4. Arnold Toynbee, *A Study of History*, vol. X, OUP 1954, pp. 130, 139–40.

5. Macmillan 1911.

6. John Wain, *Sprightly Running: Part of an Autobiography*, Macmillan 1962, pp. 35–6.

7. René Cutforth, *Order to View*, Faber & Faber 1969. This piece was first published under the title 'Illuminations' in *The Listener*, 8 February 1968. Reprinted by permission of Faber & Faber.

Chapter 12

1. C. Day Lewis, *The Buried Day*, p. 146.

2. Leonard Woolf, *Sowing: An autobiography of the years 1880–1904*, The Hogarth Press 1960, pp. 39, 41.

3. Thomas Traherne, *Centuries of Meditation*: The Third Century, No. 23.

4. *The Prelude* (1850), Book XII, lines 225–61.

5. Hugh L'Anson Fausset, *A Modern Prelude*, p. 144.

6. Colin Wilson, *Religion and the Rebel*, Victor Gollancz 1952, p. 23.

7. Bertrand Russell, *The Autobiography of Bertrand Russell*, Allen & Unwin 1967, vol. 1 1872–1914, pp. 145f.

8. T. S. Eliot, *The Dry Salvages* III.

9. Charles E. Raven, *A Wanderer's Way*, p. 63.

10. *The Autobiography of J. M. Synge*, pp. 21–2.

11. John Addington Symonds, *A Biography*, p. 19.

12. *The Autobiography of Mark Rutherford*, pp. 133–4.

13. Leo Tolstoy, *A Confession*, 1882; OUP World's Classics edition, pp. 18ff.

14. W. H. Hudson, *Far Away and Long Ago*, J. M. Dent 1936, p. 197.

15. John Casson, *Lewis and Sybil*, Collins 1972, p. 208.